Routledge Revivals

The Burial of the Dead

First published in 1920, *The Burial of the Dead* emerged from the idea that the primitive man did not imagine graves as receptacles for the dead, but refuges for the living. The book is an anthropological and a philosophical quest to understand when and how the custom of burial came about within primitive society. The book does not limit itself to the customs and traditions of burial, but also engages with the concepts of death, life, and afterlife as conceived by the primitive man. In doing so, the author traces a continuity between the strength of beliefs in a primitive society and in a modern one, as well as the development of those beliefs into universal principles. This book will be of interest to anyone trying to unravel the mystery of death and especially to students of anthropology, history, philosophy and religion.

I0127543

The Burial of the Dead

W. H. F. Basevi

Routledge
Taylor & Francis Group

First published in 1920
by George Routledge and Sons

This edition first published in 2022 by Routledge
4 Park Square, Milton Park, Abingdon, Oxon, OX14 4RN
and by Routledge
605 Third Avenue, New York, NY 10017

Routledge is an imprint of the Taylor & Francis Group, an informa business

© George Routledge and Sons 1920

Publisher's Note
The publisher has gone to great lengths to ensure the quality of this reprint but points out that some imperfections in the original copies may be apparent.

Disclaimer
The publisher has made every effort to trace copyright holders and welcomes correspondence from those they have been unable to contact.

A Library of Congress record exists under LCCN: 21009148

ISBN: 978-1-032-34933-6 (hbk)
ISBN: 978-1-003-32462-1 (ebk)
ISBN: 978-1-032-34954-1 (pbk)

Book DOI 10.4324/9781003324621

The Burial of the Dead

BY

W. H. F. BASEVI

"*Mourir, c'est simplement émigrer.*"—A. LE BRAZ.

LONDON :
GEORGE ROUTLEDGE AND SONS, LTD.
NEW YORK: E. P. DUTTON & Co.

1920

Lo, the poor Indian ! whose untutor'd mind
Sees God in clouds or hears him in the wind ;
His soul proud science never taught to stray
Far as the solar walk, or milky way ;
Yet simple nature to his hope has given,
Behind the cloud-topt hill an humbler heav'n ;
Some safer world in depth of woods embrac'd,
Some happier island in the wat'ry waste,
Where slaves once more their native land behold,
No friends torment, no Christians thirst for gold.
To Be, contents his natural desire,
He asks no angel's wing, no seraph's fire ;
But thinks, admitted to that equal sky,
His faithful dog shall bear him company.

POPE, *Essay on Man.*

CONTENTS.

CHAPTER   PAGE

PREFACE iv

INTRODUCTION v

I. THE CAVE OF AURIGNAC 1

II. THE JOURNEY OF THE DEAD . . . 19

III. FUNERAL OFFERINGS 28

IV. ORIENTATION OF GRAVES . . . 37

V. THE LAND OF THE DEAD . . . 45

VI. LOST ATLANTIS 60

VII. UNDERGROUND REGIONS OF THE DEAD . 66

VIII. DWELLINGS AND GRAVES 75

IX. THE BRETON LAND OF THE DEAD . . 88

X. CHANGE AND FORGETTING . . . 96

XI. THE LIFE OF THE DEAD . . . 104

XII. FUNERAL OFFERINGS 127

XIII. GHOSTS 138

XIV. ANCESTOR WORSHIP 155

XV. CONCURRENT METHODS OF BURIAL . . 164

XVI. TREE BURIAL 170

XVII. MOURNING 178

XVIII. RELICS OF VOLUNTARY OUTLAWRY . . 189

XIX. PRISONS 194

XX. CONCLUSION 197

PREFACE.

THE seed from which this volume sprang was a short article suggesting that the custom of placing funeral offerings in graves originated in some remote period when graves were not receptacles for the dead, but refuges for the living. It was offered to the Folk-Lore Society in the hope that others better qualified than I might prove it false or true. It was rejected without comment.

But it seemed to me that, if my interpretation of the mystery were right, its effects would be so far reaching, and it would cast new light on so many points now shrouded in obscurity, that it deserved to be followed to its logical conclusion. So I determined, though ill equipped for so venturesome an enterprise, to elaborate the theme as best I might.

It grew, almost of its own vitality, and often in directions that had not been foreseen, throwing out tentacles that grasped at things seemingly quite foreign to it ; and ever and again it showed a tendency to wander into regions where, perhaps, it is wiser not to follow until its main principle has stood the test of independent criticism.

W. H. F. B.

Darjeeling.

INTRODUCTION.

Divested of all the strange beliefs and rites that cluster round the burial of the dead, the fact alone that men adopted the custom of burial is in itself a mystery. The disposal of a dead body, in almost all cases, involves a great deal of trouble. What pressing need was it that urged primitive men with utterly inadequate tools to spend their time and labour in digging graves, making canoes, or hollowing out the trunks of trees, all for no purpose but to contain a dead body ? In sparsely populated lands, or among nomad tribes, a dead body was no danger to the living, and might well have been left uncared for, as animals leave their dead. Man once was purely animal. At what period of his progress did he begin to preserve the dead bodies of his fellows ? And what made him do it ?

It is a legitimate assumption that somewhere in the indefinitely distant past man did not bury his dead. It does not matter how far back we place this period, when he was emerging from the purely animal stage, or when he first began to use primitive implements—at some period or another he left dead bodies where they lay. What prompted those first steps in what is now a world wide custom ? or rather, from what earlier custom did it take its rise ? For customs develop from earlier customs : they do not spring fully armed from the brains of men.

Should we solve this problem we are still left face to face with another equally obscure. Why are things which are useful to the living buried with the dead ? The accepted explanation is that these offerings were made because it was believed the dead would need them. " For primitive man there was no precise break between death and life. The dead lived in the tomb (or in the Other World) the same life as he lived in this world, and it was not believed impossible that the dead could revive again." (*Folk-Lore*, vol. xxvii, p. 39.) All students are struck by these facts, and they always state them in the same way, with a want of precision that is misleading.

It is difficult to believe that early man did not know the difference between a dead man and a live one : he killed men himself, and not only killed but probably ate them. Yet we have overwhelming proof that men in a certain stage of advancement held, and do hold, beliefs similar to those mentioned. That two conflicting ideas are held simultaneously implies a mingling of two sets of facts, one at least of which is misunderstood. "I have killed my enemy and am now about to eat him," is among modern cannibals one of the elementary facts of life about which they have no illusions; and it is almost inconceivable that primitive people in past ages held less definite opinions. On the other hand, the belief that the dead in another world live the same life as they led here is founded, not on observation, but tradition. A tradition, like other things, must have had an origin, and if that origin was in the very distant past it is not surprising that misconceptions have arisen. When, therefore, it is said that "for primitive men there was no precise break between death and life," the word primitive only includes those who hold a half forgotten tradition, and we are liable to overlook the vast ages that lie behind. We have no reason to suppose that the ideas of men who lived in the far distant past were the same as those of modern savages. A great deal of thinking, of wondering and reasoning, and, what is equally important, a great deal of forgetting has gone on during those many centuries.

Unquestionably these beliefs are held by most primitive people in the present day; but we have no right to assume that their ancestors in far off times held them also. The fact that weapons and remains of food are found near dead bodies of men who undoubtedly lived in the palæolithic age is usually accepted as a proof that this was so; but, as will be seen, the facts will bear quite a different interpretation. But even if palæolithic man did hold these beliefs the problem is no nearer solution. If we go far enough back in the history of the human race, there must have been a time, even if it was when man was little more than an animal, when he did not. Then how did these ideas arise? *Ex nihil nihil fit* is as true of beliefs as of more substantial things.

Speaking of the Breton country Le Braz says: "Telles régions, d'une solitude farouche et presque sinistre, appellent nécessairement le mythe." Why, certainly! But the myth must exist before it can be called. A gloomy, solitary spot arouses the fear of meeting ghosts in the same way as a patch of marshy ground suggests the agreeable prospect of coming across snipe. In both cases it is a matter of experience, personal or traditional. People believe in ghosts because a tradition has been handed down to them that ghosts exist. It is our business to discover how the tradition took its rise.

Civilized races in the present day hold their beliefs with just the same fervour of conviction as the savage, and for precisely the same reason. Some, for example, believe intensely, even heatedly, in free-trade : the reason being that at one time, in certain conditions, free trade proved of great value to the nation. Others hold, as warmly, a belief in protection : because in certain circumstances protection proved its value. Again, there is a wide-spread and deep conviction that education is a panacea for most, if not all the troubles of the poorer classes ; because in certain circumstances a great need for educated men offered opportunities for those who had this qualification to improve their condition. These are the causes that led to the beliefs, though not the arguments by which we support them. We believe in customs that proved useful under certain conditions and we elevate them into universal principles. So the beliefs of primitive people have their roots in the customs of long ago. They appear to us absurd because we do not know the conditions in which they began. Perhaps our own beliefs may appear absurd to future generations.

Beliefs grow out of customs ; and tradition is the explanation, garbled often beyond recognition, of the purpose of those customs whose original use may since have been forgotten. For customs survive the conditions that gave rise to them, and, ceasing to be of practical use, degenerate into rites and ceremonies. These continue to be practised owing to the inherent conservatism of man who clings to anything whose value has been proved, even though it be no longer valuable. Fashions die soon that are devised only to meet temporary conditions : but those which have been effective for long ages take long ages to decay. A good custom is an asset not lightly to be cast aside. At first men believe in it because it proves useful : later on because it formerly proved useful.

Among people ignorant of written language the conditions in which their fore-fathers lived are soon forgotten, but the customs which were practised are practised still ; and tradition, becoming vaguer and more inaccurate in each succeeding generation, tells what was their purpose. But conditions having changed, that purpose is no longer intelligible. Still, the custom and the tradition are ingrained in the life of the people, forming a part of their inheritance, and ranking equal with the stock of acquired knowledge handed down to them by their ancestors. For a great lapse of time, perhaps, the custom was of proved value, and those who neglected it suffered. So men know that it was good and true ; and the belief was passed on from one generation to another hardening with age. Thus custom, tradition, and belief survive together as mysteries only to be solved by reconstructing the primitive conditions in which they were born.

Hitherto, as far as I am aware, all who have written on the subject of primitive burial, have accounted for the strange customs by assuming that they were adopted to conform with the people's ideas concerning death. " But," says Mr. Hocart (*Folk-Lore*, vol. xxvi. p. 116), " to explain a custom as the outcome of deliberate invention is to explain nothing. . . We are in no way wiser for being told that Australians deliberated at some time in the distant past, because all men are continually deliberating, only they are not always deliberating about the same objects, and therefore it is these objects that interest us by their difference, not their deliberations which are all very much alike." It is the conditions of life that compel men to adopt a custom in the first instance. If, therefore, we would understand the custom we must discover the conditions it was invented to meet.

As all attempts have failed to explain funeral customs by assuming that they were adopted to conform with primitive ideas concerning death, let us see what will result if we adopt the postulate that custom came first in point of time.

BURIAL OF THE DEAD.

CHAPTER I.

THE CAVE OF AURIGNAC.

Funeral customs throughout the world have one factor common to all : it is embodied in rites and ceremonies, and finds expression in tradition and belief. This greatest common factor is the assumption that the dead man has not ceased to live. Everywhere we find this indicated, in tradition and in practice, among races far asunder in culture, space, and time, whose manners and ceremonies have little else in common. In or near the grave are placed food, and clothes, and weapons ; while the body is protected from molestation often most elaborately. All this provision conveys the idea that there is something more in burial than the disposal of a dead man's bones. It is all so eminently practical, though so ill-timed, and so exclusively concerned with material needs as to imply—with a strange insistency, as though fearful that we might forget or fail to understand—that it is dealing with a living person.

But an implication, however strong, is very unsafe evidence of fact, and its guidance might wisely be declined were it not that belief endorses custom.   Here we find many sign-boards pointing in the same direction.   The folk-lore of many lands tells of the difficult and dangerous journey that the dead must undertake, generally alone and unprotected ; of the land where he will dwell, and the occupations he will be engaged in when at last he reaches home.   These beliefs, and many others that will be considered in their turn, are based on the assumption that the dead man is alive and will continue his existence in conditions not so very different from those that he has left.   As Le Braz puts it :   " Mourir c'est simplement émigrer."

It is unfortunately one of our many limitations that we can so rarely look at anything in life as an isolated fact, unconsciously we adulterate it with inherited beliefs.   But if we make an effort to overcome, as far as may be, our traditional bias, and, by an exercise of the imagination, try to put ourselves in the place of one who meets the facts for the first time and without any association of old ideas, we must surely be led to one inevitable conclusion : originally these ceremonies had to do with living men. Far away in past ages it was for the preservation of a living person that such careful arrangements were made : it was a weak but living person whose body needed protection : the food was placed for someone who would soon be hungry, the clothes because he would be cold, and the weapons so that he might hunt and fight. A long and perilous journey lay before him, and at the end of it he would occupy himself in much the same way as he had always done.

Thus baldly stated the conclusion may at first sight appear far fetched, presenting one apparently insuperable objection. In all the stages of his career, animal, savage, barbaric, and civilized, man has been always in close touch with death. What, then, could have induced him to treat his dead as though they were alive ? Even if, as has been claimed, these funeral ceremonies were originally carried out for the benefit of a living person, it is by no means clear what purpose they were intended to accomplish. But supposing we admit for the sake of argument that they did serve some useful purpose, there still remains the apparently unanswerable question : if these things at first were done for the good of the living, how did it come about in later times, that they were carried out to benefit the dead ? The accepted explanation is that given by Pope and, since, by many other writers. We expect to meet it in every book on anthropology we open, and we are rarely disappointed. Because, for the last few thousand years, the races of men have believed in an existence after death, it has been assumed that the same belief was current in prehistoric times and was the reason for all the trouble taken about a dead man's body. This is pure assumption : fiction unsupported by a single fact.

As has just been stated, the problem is a double one : What conditions of primitive life were these preparations first intended to meet ? And how did it come about that what was once done for the living was afterwards done for the dead ? These questions will be answered in the order they arise, and I now venture on somewhat dangerous ground in an endeavour to reconstruct those past conditions leaving future chapters to show whether the evidence is sufficient to prove the case. But first I will quote at con- siderable length Lyell's description of a Palæo- lithic grave.

BURIAL-PLACE AT AURIGNAC, IN THE SOUTH
OF FRANCE, OF PLEISTOCENE DATE.[1]

" I have alluded in the beginning of the fourth
chapter to a custom prevalent among rude
nations of consigning to the tomb works of art,
once the property of the dead, or objects of their
affection, and even of storing up, in many cases,
animal food destined for the manes of the defunct
in the future life. I also cited M. Desnoyers'
comments on the absence among the bones
of wild and domestic animals found in old Gaulish
Tombs of all inter-mixture of extinct species of
quadrupeds, as proving that the oldest sepulchral
monuments then known in France (1845) had no
claims to high antiquity founded on palæonto-
logical data.

" M. Lartet, however, has recently published
a circumstantial account of what seems clearly
to have been a sepulchral vault of the Pleistocene
period, near Aurignac, not far from the foot of
the Pyrenees. I have had the advantage of
inspecting the fossil bones and works of art
obtained by him from that grotto, and of con-
versing and corresponding with him on the
subject, and can see no grounds for doubting
the soundness of his conclusions.

[1] Lyell's *Antiquity of Man*, chap. x.

" The town of Aurignac is situated in the department of the Haute Garonne, near a spur of the Pyrenees ; adjoining it is the small flat-topped hill of Fajoles, about 60 feet above the brook called Rodes, which flows at its foot on one side. It consists of Nummulitic limestone, presenting a steep escarpment towards the north-west, on which side in the face of the rock, about 45 feet above the brook, is now visible the entrance of a grotto a, which opened originally on the terrace h, c, k, which slopes gently towards the valley.

" Until the year 1852, the opening into this grotto was masked by a talus of small fragments of limestone and earthy matter e, such as the rain may have washed down the slope of the hill. In that year a labourer named Bonnemaison, employed in repairing roads, observed that rabbits, when hotly pursued by the sportsman, ran into a hole which they had burrowed in the talus, at $i f$. On reaching as far into the opening as the length of his arm, he drew out, to his surprise, one of the long bones of the human skeleton ; and his curiosity being excited, and having a suspicion that the hole communicated with a subterranean cavity, he commenced digging a trench through the middle of the talus, and in a few hours found himself opposite a large

heavy slab of rock *f h,* placed vertically against
the entrance. Having removed this, he discovered on the other side of it an arched cavity

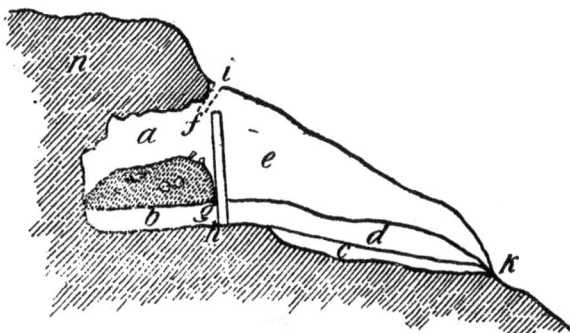

Section of part of the hill of Fajoles passing through
the sepulchral grotto of Aurignac.

(*a*) Part of the vault in which the remains of seventeen
human skeletons were found.

(*b*) Layer of made ground, two feet thick, inside the grotto
in which a few human bones, with entire bones of extinct
and living species of animals, and many works of art were
embedded.

(*c*) Layers of ashes and charcoal, six inches thick, with
broken, burnt, and gnawed bones of extinct and recent
mammalia ; also hearth-stones and works of art ; no human
bones.

(*d*) Deposits with similar contents and a few scattered
cinders.

(*e*) Talus of rubbish washed down from the hill above.

(*f g*) Slab of rock which closed the vault, not ascertained
whether it extended to *h.*

(*f i*) Rabbit burrow which led to the discovery of the grotto.

(*h k*) Original terrace on which the grotto opened.

(*n*) Nummulitic limestone of hill of Fajoles.

a. 7 or 8 feet in its greatest height, 10 in width,
and 7 in horizontal depth. It was almost filled
with bones, among which were two entire skulls

which he recognised at once as human. The people of Aurignac, astonished to hear of the occurrence of so many human relics in so lonely a spot, flocked to the cave, and Dr. Amiel, the Mayor, ordered all the bones to be taken out and reinterred in the parish cemetery. But before this was done, having as a medical man a knowledge of anatomy, he ascertained by counting the homologous bones that they must have formed parts of no less than seventeen skeletons of both sexes, and all ages ; some so young that the ossification of some of the bones was incomplete. Unfortunately the skulls were injured in the transfer ; and what is worse, after the lapse of eight years, when M. Lartet visited Aurignac, the village sexton was unable to tell him in what exact place the trench was dug, into which the skeletons had been thrown, so that their rich harvest of ethnological knowledge seems for ever lost to the antiquary and geologist.

" M. Lartet having been shown, in 1860, the remains of some extinct animals and works of art, found in digging the original trench made by Bonnemaison through the bed *d* under the talus, and some others brought out from the interior of the grotto, determined to investigate systematically what remained intact of the deposits outside and inside the vault, those inside, underlying the human skeletons, being supposed to consist entirely of made ground. Having obtained the assistance of some intelligent workmen, he personally superintended their labours, and found outside the grotto, resting on the sloping terrace *h k*, the layer of ashes and charcoal *c*, about 6 inches thick, extending over an area of 6 or 7 square yards, and going as far as the entrance of the grotto and no farther, there being no cinders or charcoal in the interior. Among the cinders outside the vault were fragments of fissile sandstone, reddened by heat, which were observed to rest on a levelled surface of Nummulitic limestone and to have formed a hearth. The nearest place from whence such slabs of sandstone could have been brought was the opposite side of the valley.

" Among the ashes, and in some overlying earthy layers, *d*, separating the ashes from the talus *e*, were a great variety of bones and implements ; amongst the latter not fewer than a hundred flint articles—knives, projectiles, sling stones, and chips, and among them one of those siliceous cores or nuclei with numerous facets, from which flint flakes or knives had been struck off, seeming to prove that some instruments were occasionally manufactured on the very spot.

" Among other articles outside the entrance was found a stone of a circular form, and flattened on two sides, with a central depression, composed of a tough rock which does not belong to that region of the Pyrenees. This instrument is supposed by the Danish antiquaries to have been used for removing by skilful blows the edges of flint knives, the fingers and thumb being placed in the two opposite depressions during the operation. Among the bone instruments were arrows without barbs, and other tools made of reindeer horn, and a bodkin formed out of the more compact horn of the roedeer. This instrument was well shaped, and sharply pointed, and in so good a state of preservation that it might still be used for piercing the tough skins of animals.

" Scattered through the same ashes and earth were the bones of various species of animals. The bones of the herbivora were the most numerous, and all those on the outside of the grotto which had contained marrow were invariably split open as if for its extraction, many of them being also burnt. The spongy parts, moreover, were wanting, having been eaten off and gnawed after they were broken, the work, according to M. Lartet, of hyænas, the bones and coprolites of which were mixed with the cinders, and dispersed through the over-lying soil *d*. The beasts of prey are supposed to have prowled about the spot and fed on such relics of the funeral feasts as remained after the retreat of the human visitors, or during the intervals between successive funeral cere-monies which accompanied the interment of the corpses within the sepulchre. Many of the bones were also streaked as if the flesh had been scraped off by a flint instrument

" Among the various proofs that the bones were fresh when brought to the spot, it is remarked that those of the herbivora not only bore the marks of having had the marrow extracted and having afterwards been gnawed and in part devoured as if by carnivorous beasts, but that they had also been acted upon by fire (and this was especially noticed in one case of a cavebear's bone), in such a manner as to show that they retained in them at the time all their animal matter.

" Among other quadrupeds which appear to have been eaten at the funeral feasts, and of which the bones occurred among the ashes, were those of a young *Rhinoceros tichorhinus*, the bones of which had been, like those of the accompany-ing herbivora, broken and gnawed by a beast of prey at both extremities

" Outside the great slab of stone forming the door, not one human bone occurred ; inside of it there were found, mixed with loose soil, the remains of as many as seventeen human individuals, besides some works of art and bones of animals.   We know nothing of the arrangement of these bones when they were first broken into. M. Lartet inferred at first that the bodies were bent down upon themselves in a squatting attitude, a posture known to have been adopted in most of the sepulchres of primitive times ; but this opinion he has since retracted.

" Mixed with the human bones inside the grotto first removed by Bonnemaison, were eighteen small, round, and flat plates of a white shelly substance, made of some species of cockle (*Cardium*), pierced through the middle as if for being strung into a bracelet. In the substratum also in the interior examined by M. Lartet was found the tusk of a young *Ursus spelosus*, the crown of which had been stripped of its enamel, and which had been carved perhaps in imitation of the head of a bird. It was perforated lengthwise as if for suspension as an ornament or amulet. A flint knife also was found in the interior which had evidently never been used ; in this respect, unlike the numerous worn specimens found outside, so that it is conjectured that it may, like other associated works of art, have been placed there as part of the funeral ceremonies.

" A few teeth of the cave-lion, *Felis spelœa*, and two tusks of the wild boar, also found in the interior, were memorials perhaps of the chase. No remains of the same animals were met with among the external relics.

" On the whole, the bones of animals inside the vault offer a remarkable contrast to those of the exterior, being all entire and uninjured, none of them broken, gnawed, half-eaten, scraped, or burnt like those lying among the ashes on the other side of the great slab which formed the portal. The bones of the interior seem to have been clothed with their flesh when buried in the layer of loose soil strewed over the floors. In confirmation of this idea, many bones of the skeleton were often observed to be in juxta-position, and in one spot all the bones of the leg of an *Ursus spelæus* were lying together uninjured. Add to this, the entire absence in the interior of cinders and charcoal and we can scarcely doubt that we have here an example of an ancient place of sepulture, closed at the opening so effectually against the hyænas or other carnivora that no marks of their teeth appear on any of the bones, whether human or brute.

" The Aurignac cave adds no new species to the list of extinct quadrupeds, which we have elsewhere, and by independent evidence, ascertained to have once flourished contemporaneously with man. But if the fossil memorials have been correctly interpreted—if we have here before us at the northern base of the Pyrenees a sepulchral vault with skeletons of human beings, consigned by friends and relatives to their last resting-place—if we have also at the portal of the tomb the relics of funeral feasts, and within it indications of viands destined for the use of the departed on their way to a land of spirits ; while among the funeral gifts are weapons wherewith in other fields to chase the gigantic deer, the cave-lion, the cave-bear, and woolly rhinoceros—we have at last succeeded in tracing back the sacred rites of burial, and, more interesting still, a belief in a future state, to times long anterior to those of history and tradition. Rude and superstitious as may have been the savage of that remote era, he still deserves by cherishing hopes of a hereafter, the epithet of ' noble,' which Dryden gave to what he seems to have pictured to himself as the primitive conditon of our race,

' As Nature first made man
When wild in woods the noble savage ran.' "

It will be observed that Lyell, who in matters of geology displays the doubting mind of Thomas, accepts unquestioningly the Poets' theory of the origin of burial.

I will now endeavour to depict the scene enacted at this grotto—or, rather, one of many scenes, for it is clear that the cave was often used. Imagination is a treacherous guide but, like the blind man's dog, it is all we have to lead us ; so when venturing off the beaten track we must be careful to test each step as we go, tapping the ground with the blind man's stick. Although my story may appear at first too fanciful for serious consideration, later chapters will, I think, establish the probability of its main features.

A band of hunters of the palæolithic age are returning from the chase laden with the carcasses of animals they have trapped or killed. One of them has been severely injured by some wild beast, or perhaps in battle, and the progress of the party is delayed. Far distant is the cave where their women and children are awaiting their return, and these will starve if food does not reach them soon. Burdened with quantities of flesh the little band is in danger, not only from carnivorous animals, but also from any other band of hungry hunters they may encounter. So haste is imperative, and yet their wounded companion cannot hurry. Had he been old, or useless, or injured beyond hope of recovery, they would no doubt have left him to his fate ; for life was hard and men were ruthless. But except for his wound, which will heal in time, he is a strong and vigorous man, a skilful hunter, and a cunning and intrepid warrior. So, in the interest of the tribe, all that is possible must be done to save him. One of the party notices a cave in the hill side which precisely meets their needs, so they halt there for a while. Some collect wood and make a fire to cook their food, some go down to the stream and bring back water in hollow horns and skulls,[1] while others search for a rock to cover the mouth of the cave in which their wounded friend is resting. Then they feed together round the fire. Having eaten their fill they put a store of food and water inside the cave, enough to last their friend for several days. They give him his weapons : they place the rock against the cave mouth to keep out wolves and hyænas ; and then they leave him and resume their homeward journey. If he recovers before his stock of food and water is exhausted he will push away the rock, issue from the cave with his

[1] The use of skulls as cups is often recorded in folk-tales. " Milk drunk from the skull of Conall Cernach restored to enfeebled warriors their pristine strength. . . . There is a folk survival in the Highlands of drinking from the skull of a suicide." McCulloch, *Religion of the Ancient Celts*, p. 241.

weapons in his hand, and follow in their tracks. But if he dies, his bones, unless disturbed by other palæolithic men, will lie there for ten thousand years until some archæologist unearths the ' grave ' and assumes that he was buried.

This, or some ' such custom, varied to suit different needs, I take to be the original from which all modes of burial took their rise. How it came about that a device for protecting the living was adopted as a method of disposing of the dead will be the subject of investigation later. Also we shall see how people came to forget that the custom originally had nothing to do with dead men. Yet people have not quite forgotten even now, for in all current beliefs there lies an implication that the corpse is playing the part, so to speak, of a living person. Meanwhile we have an explanation of these ancient graves, so called, which accounts for their existence, and for the relics found in and round them, without demanding that their inmates were dead when buried, or that the makers of the graves had formulated theories of a future life and the resurrection of the body.

And yet another difficulty vanishes that has never been adequately met. If in those very early times burial was the general method of disposing of the dead, how is it that so few graves

have been discovered ?   This difficulty has always
been glossed over.   After a few vague phrases
about the paucity of the population, and the
imperfection of the geological record, the matter
has been thrust aside.   Yet even though the
population at any given time was small, the
number of generations was immense, and,
especially where cave-burial was practiced, we
might reasonably expect to find numerous
remains, even after allowing for the wearing away
of hills, alterations in the course of rivers and
other geological changes.   But if the dead were
not buried until comparatively recent times,
if these palæolithic ' graves ' were merely shelters
for men who were temporarily disabled and
might reasonably be expected to recover, we at
once reduce our figures.   It was not the millions
of the old, as age then went, not the very ill,
the maimed, the decrepit, and the dying, but
only the slightly injured who were cared for,
and those suffering from an illness not usually
fatal, and the majority of these soon left the
refuge.   It was only when the diagnosis was
wrong and the sick man died that a record
remained for discovery in future ages.

CHAPTER II.

THE JOURNEY OF THE DEAD.

THE LYKE WAKE DIRGE OF THE NORTH COUNTRY.[1]

> This a nighte, this a nighte,
>   Every night and alle ;
> Fire and fleet and candle-light,
>   And Christe receive thy saule.
>
> When thou from hence away are paste,
>   Every night and alle ;
> To Whinny-moor thou comes at laste.
>   And Christe receive thy saule.
>
> From Whinny-moor when thou may passe
>   Every night and alle ;
> To Brig o' Dread thou comes at laste,
>   And Christe receive thy saule.

In the first chapter a passing reference was made to the popular belief that the dead man has to undertake a journey. This belief is so wide spread as to be practically universal ; in fact it is the dominant note in custom and tradition almost throughout the world. As far as I am aware it is only in Brittany, for reasons which will be considered later, that the journey of the

[1] *Glossary of Cleveland Dialect*, J. C. Atkinson. Also quoted with slight variations in *Curiosities of Indo-European Tradition and Folk-Lore*, by Walter K. Kelly, p. 116 (Chapman and Hall, 1863).

soul takes a very secondary place. The belief is so well known that it would be a waste of time to dwell upon the subject were it not intimately connected with the tradition of a Land of the Dead and with the strange but common practice of orienting graves. Both these matters have recently been the subject of interesting speculation by Mr. W. J. Perry[1] who has arrived at surprisingly correct results, and, had his argument not been deflected by a bias towards what I have called the Poets' theory, he would perhaps have solved the mystery.

Here again, as in the previous chapter, I must assume, what later on I hope to prove, that this tradition in its origin was not concerned in any way with death. These epics of travel, recorded often in great detail, and with such simple and convincing realism, were the experiences of living men—true travellers' tales. But in the form that they have reached us, curtailed and condensed in the lapse of centuries, they resemble a newspaper review of some book of sport and exploration where a general summary is interspersed with extracts and explanations. As the reviewer has not done the journey himself and may not understand what he has read, his explanations

[1] Myths of Origin and the Home of the Dead in Indonesia. *Folk-Lore*, vol. xxvi., pp. 138 *et seq.*

sometimes are misleading. So it has happened with traditions. Succeeding generations when passing on the tale have added their own interpretation to things that were not clear to them. The traditions of the Journey of the Dead is a very good example, and in due course the misunderstanding will be explained. Meantime it is enough to say that it was due to reason working on facts that were not understood. Man reasons always in the same way, and the facts available were everywhere much the same, hence the results bear that resemblance throughout the world which causes such surprise.

A few examples will suffice to indicate the general tenor of these stories whose interesting features will be the subject of more detailed investigation in future chapters. The typical features are summed up in the Handbook of Folk-Lore. Very frequently there is " the crossing of a river, lake, or sea ; an idea deeply rooted in popular Protestant phraseology, though not found in either the Old or New Testament Scriptures. Bunyan's Pilgrims forded the river of death : Roman shades were ferried across by Charon : faithful Mohammedans reach their Paradise by a bridge formed of a single hair. The wild tribes of the Malay Peninsular imagine a fallen tree-trunk bridging a boiling lake . . .

and Yorkshire peasants of the seventeenth century used to sing a funeral dirge recounting the perils of the soul's journey over Whinny muir (the furzy moor) and across ' the Brig o' Dread, nae brader than a thread.'

As a side issue it is interesting to note how the Protestants of northern Europe have retained their old tradition of pagan times and woven it into the intrusive Christian faith. It shows how hard it is to obliterate the memories of the past. But more interesting still is the realism of these recorded journeys whose dangers, difficulties, and hardships have burned themselves into the memory of men. In the present day, if we exclude the arctic and antarctic regions, wherever civilized explorers go they find aborigines who know the way. Everywhere there are well known, if not well beaten, tracks. But even now there is one point where reports of modern explorers are strangely similar to tradition. The ' fallen tree trunk,' the bridge ' formed by a single hair,' or ' no broader than a thread ' : how these terms recall the descriptions which travellers give us of bridges in Thibet, and Western China, and Peru !

The difficulty of crossing rivers is a topic that recurs frequently. The Hindu will often die grasping a cow's tail as if to swim across the

Vaitarani in herdsman's fashion, holding on to a cow.[1] The Choctaws believe that souls journey westwards, and a long, slippery pine-log, stretching from hill to hill, bridges over a deep and dreadful river.[2] The bridge-myth survives also in an Irish poem which speaks of the *drochet bethad*, or bridge of-life, and in the *drochaid na flaitheanas*, or bridge of heaven, of Hebridean folk-lore.[3]. Sometimes it is a lake or sea that has to be crossed. At the extreme western cape of Vanua Levu, a calm and solemn place of cliff and forest, the souls of the Fijian dead embark for the judgment seat of Ndengei, and thither the living come in pilgrimage, thinking to see their ghosts and gods.[4] Irish and Breton folk-lore teams with such stories. According to Egyptian belief the soul (Ba) travelled to the Kingdom of Seker or Osiris or joined the god Ra. It stopped to refresh itself at a sycamore tree, then traversed a desert interspersed with marshes, where serpents and wild beasts abounded, until it reached a lake across which it was ferried to some islands. According to another account the soul travels west to Abydos whence it proceeds by boat to the realms of Osiris.

[1] Tylor, *Primitive Culture*, vol. i., 473.
[2] *idem*, vol. ii., 94.
[3] MacCullock, *Religion of the Ancient Celts*, chap. xv., 228.
[4] Tylor, *Primitive Culture*, vol. ii., p. 45.

These few examples, taken at random, show how the difficulties and dangers of travelling in early times impressed themselves on the human memory. But it is not a matter for surprise that tradition still records them, for it was only very slowly and gradually, as man increased and multiplied, that he was able to subdue the earth by making roads, building bridges, and exterminating noxious animals. Even in the most civilized parts of Europe this has only been accomplished within the historical period, while in many parts of the world the process has scarcely yet begun.

These examples have been quoted, not for the purpose of explaining, what indeed is self-evident, that travelling in prehistoric times was more difficult than now, but because of their bearing on subjects that will be considered later. The stories quoted all imply that they recount real journeys, journeys therefore that were made by living men ; and the chapters that follow next will show what great care and forethought men displayed in providing against the trials that lay before them.

There are three points of view from which descriptions of the dead man's journey must be regarded—always remembering that originally he was not dead—and it is necessary to keep them quite distinct ; for all appear to be recorded in tradition causing sometimes an apparent contradiction, or at least a confusion of ideas. But though they often overlap or merge into each other there still remains sufficient evidence to indicate their separate origin.

First comes the incident already mentioned when a hunting or raiding party had to leave behind an injured comrade. A record of this was preserved among the Algonquin tribes when a public address was made to the body at burial concerning its future path. One can almost see this being done—how many thousand years ago ?—outside the grotto at Aurignac before the heavy stone was raised to close the entrance.

Next we must consider those, the women, children, and infirm, who were left behind in safety when the young men set out to hunt for food. This also is recorded in the customs of some tribes, the lost companion being represented by a living person. " Thirty days after the death of an adult Musquakie Indian the dead man is personated by a friend, who in this character attends a farewell feast. . . . He is called the ghost-carrier. When the sun goes down he departs towards the west, convoyed by a number of friends of the deceased, all of whom, like himself, are painted. After night-fall

they return and are welcomed as from a long
journey. The ghost-carrier is addressed by the
name of the deceased. In a few days he visits
the parents of the deceased, announcing himself
as their dead son who will take care of them in
their old age.[1] " In this we seem to have a
clear representation of the return of the injured
man after his recovery. It is true that he
returns with his companions after night-fall,
but this is probably for convenience and not as
part of the ceremony, for it is not until a few days
later that he visits the parents of his deceased
friend,

One other class of facts remains that has not
yet been touched on. When communities
migrated, whether they were great or small,
similar incidents must often have occurred.
But the customs which record this state of things
contain such special features that they demand
a chapter to themselves. The ceremonies that
deal with these events are very numerous, for in
early times migration, though on a small scale,
was not merely frequent but continuous.

Among a population mainly pastoral migration
is often, even in the present day, an annual
necessity. In Switzerland and Norway the cattle
that have spent the winter stabled in the valleys

[1] Owen, *Folk-Lore of the Musquakie Indians*, 81.

are driven to the hills in summer for the grazing. In Western India the shepherds spend the winter months in Sind, but when the hot weather commences they drive their flocks into the high lands of Baluchistan. If we cast back to more primitive times we find the same need to move, though for different reasons. The Andamanese neither cultivate the soil nor keep domestic animals, but hunt and fish and search for grubs and roots. In order to find sufficient food they are kept in a constant state of movement, travelling from place to place as supplies become exhausted. It has been ascertained that their movements resemble those of migratory birds. They have a number of halting places that they visit in rotation. Somewhat similar appears to have been the habit of those ancient tribes whose kitchen middens in Denmark have been the object of much detailed investigation.

In less favoured parts of the world drought, as we know, drives the population from one spot to another ; while disease, dangerous animals, and the pressure of hostile tribes have similar results. Over population may be left aside for the present, though it will not be overlooked, for the phenomena to which it gives rise are more noticeable in the agricultural stage of advancement.

CHAPTER III.

So, hush ! I will give you this leaf to keep :
See, I shut it inside the sweet cold hand !
There, that is our secret : go to sleep !
You will wake, and remember, and understand.

The assumption, for it is nothing more, that graves were always graves has led mankind to speculate wildly about the purpose of funeral offerings. Anthropologists have added another assumption to the first and then proceeded to discuss the situation with gravity and much learning. For example Tylor says, and many other writers have followed his lead, " A wide survey of funeral sacrifices over the world will plainly show one of their most usual motives to be a more or less defined notion of benefiting the deceased, whether out of kindness to him or from fear of his displeasure."[1]   So far so good : he observes and states a fact.   But he then goes on to say, quoting Alger, " The barbarian brain seems to have been generally impregnated with the feeling that everything else has a ghost as

[1] Tylor, *Primitive Culture,* vol. i., p. 484.

well as man. . . . . The custom of burning or burying things with the dead probably arose, in some cases at least, from the supposition that every object has its *manes*."[1] The fallacy is due to the inversion of cause and effect : beliefs arise from customs, not customs from beliefs

The assumption made by primitive people throughout the world is that offerings made at graves are for the use of a dead man. With nothing but custom and tradition to guide them they could arrive at no other conclusion ; for they have no knowledge of the gradual change which caused a refuge for the weak to be employed for the disposal of the dead, nor of the phenomenon that custom outlives its usefulness. By the natural process of enquiry they would ask : Why is food given to the dead unless to eat, clothes to wear, and weapons except to hunt and fight with ? Then tradition stepping in fixed them in their error by telling of a journey and a Land of the Dead.

Where modern writers have failed is in taking the ' untutored savage ' of the present day as a true representative of primeval man, forgetting that savages, like more civilized races, have developed in the course of time, though not so

[1] Tylor. *Primitive Culture*, vol. i.. p. 484, quoting Alger, *Future Life*, p. 81.

far, nor often in the same directions. We have no right to assume, we have every reason not to assume, that living men, civilized or savage, are in the same mental state as their ancestors. Not that the human brain has developed, but because the accumulated experience of ages has taught them things unknown to their forefathers, while, on the other hand, ancient methods, designed to meet the needs of former times, having been superceded, their intention has passed out of knowledge.

So it has been with funeral offerings. In the first chapter I indicated, what I hope to prove in due course, that graves originally were refuges for the weak, and what are now funeral offerings were nothing more nor less than the means of subsistence and defence. In course of time these very shelters, or others of like kind, ceased to be used as refuges, and became depositories for dead bodies. But though the dead instead of the sick were consigned to these caves and grottos, the custom connected with the act, that is to say the provision of food and weapons, was not discontinued, and tradition—becoming more vague in each succeeding generation—explained that they were for the dead man's use. All this, of course, implies that the change in habits was very gradual as men adapted themselves to slowly changing conditions. But this —like other practices that once were useful— when it became useless crystallized into a rite sanctified by immemorial custom.

It will now be clear why certain kinds of offerings were made, such as food and weapons; and, once the original intention was forgotten, it is not difficult to understand that the practice would develop to include many other things that were useful to people in a more advanced stage of culture.

"Over the whole Celtic area a rich profusion of grave-goods has been found, consisting of weapons, armour, chariots, utensils, ornaments, and coins."[1] Among the Algonquin tribes the sacrifice of objects for the dead was a habitual rite, as when we read of a warrior's corpse being buried with musket and war-club, calumet and war-paint.[2] Turanian tribes of North Asia avow that the motive of their funeral offerings of horses and sledges, clothes and axes and kettles, flint and· steel and tinder, meat and butter, is to provide the dead for his journey to the land of souls, and for his life there. Among the Esths of Northern Europe, the dead starts properly equipped on his ghostly journey with

[1] MacCullock, *The Religion of the Ancient Celts*, xxii., 337.
[2] Tylor, *Primitive Culture*, vol. i., p. 181.

needle and thread, hairbrush and soap, bread
and brandy and coin. Among the Orang Binua
of Sambawa there prevails this curious law of
inheritance ;   not only does each surviving
relative, father, mother, son, brother, and so
forth, take his or her proper share, but the
deceased inherits one share from himself, which
is devoted to his use by eating the animals at
the funeral feast. burning everything else that
will burn, and burying the remainder.[1]   Just
as people in Borneo, after they had become
Mohammedans, still kept up the rite of burying
provisions for the dead man's journey, as a mark
of respect, so the rite of interring funeral offerings
survived in Christian Europe.   The ancient Greek
burial of the dead with the obolus in his mouth
for Charon's toll is represented in the modern
Greek world, where Charon and the funeral
coin are both familiar. As the old Prussians
furnished the dead with spending-money to buy
refreshment on his weary journey, so to this
day German peasants bury a corpse with money
in his mouth or hand. Similar little funeral
offerings of coin are recorded in the folk-lore books
elsewhere in Europe.[2]   " The Tunguz has buried
with him his horse, his bow and arrows, his

[1] Tylor Primiti e Culture, vol. i., p. 483.
[2] Tylor. Primitive Culture, vol. i., p. 494.

smoking apparatus and kettle. The Australian
will take his weapons with him to paradise.
A Tasmanian, asked the reason of a spear being
deposited in a native grave replied ' To fight
with when he is asleep.' Many Greenlanders
thought that the arrows and tools laid by a dead
man's grave would be used in the next world.
The instruments buried with the Sioux are for
him to make a living with hereafter. The paints
provided for the dead Iroquois were to enable
him to appear decently in the other world. The
Aztec's water-bottle was to serve him on the
journey to Mictlan, the land of the dead.
Turanian tribes of North Asia avow that the
motive of their funeral offerings of horses and
sledges, clothes and axes etc. is to provide the
dead for his journey to the land of souls, and
for his life there."[1] " The Pawnee warrior's
horse is slain on his grave to be ready for him to
mount again, and the Comanche's best horses
are buried with his favourite weapons and his
pipe, all alike to be used in the distant happy
hunting grounds. Patagonian tribes bury with
the deceased his arms and ornaments and even
kill on his tomb all the animals which belonged
to him, that he may find them in the abode of
bliss. The dead Buraet's favourite horse, led

[1] *Ibid*, vol. i., p. 486, *et seq.*

C

saddled to the grave killed and flung in, may
serve for a Tartar example. Germany retained
the sacrifice until quite recent times. A Cavalry
General, Count Friedrich Kasimir Boos von
Waldeck, was buried at Treves in 1781 according
to the forms of the Teutonic order ; his horse
was led in the procession, and the coffin having
been lowered into the grave the horse was killed
and thrown in upon it. This was, perhaps,
the last occasion when such a sacrifice was con-
summated in solemn form in Europe. But that
pathetic incident of a soldier's funeral, the leading of the saddled and bridled charger in the
mournful procession, keeps up to this day a
lingering reminiscence of the grim religious rite
now passed away."[1]

The examples quoted do not cover all forms
of funeral offerings and sacrifices. They
represent only those connected with a very
primitive stage of man's career with additions
due, as has just been explained, to an extension
of the idea when the meaning of the ceremony
was forgotten. Other examples, illustrating a
more advanced state of culture, are given in
chapter eight. Those now mentioned, with the
light that has been thrown on the subject in the
first chapter, need no explanation—except

[1] Tylor, *Primitive Culture*, vol. i., p. 472, *et seq.*

perhaps the incident of the slaughter of a horse, and even this offers little difficulty when it is remembered that in all likelihood man ate horses long before he learned to ride or drive them.

A problem, however, faces us now that did not arise over the evolution of shelters into graves. Graves developed from shelters by a natural extension of the original idea. The injured man did not always recover ; so when population increased, migration became less frequent, and dead bodies had to be disposed of somehow, it was no strange thing to put the dead where men had died. An old custom was adapted to meet a new need, which is the usual highroad to progress. In both instances, too, the need was a practical one.

Now, however, we come to a gap between the old and the new. Grave-goods, as we have just seen, were intended for the support and protection of a living man. Funeral offerings are given to the dead. Though the old custom has been retained, the motive is a new one. It is no longer concerned with the practical needs of this life, but with the belief in a future existence. It is between these two different sets of ideas that the hiatus occurs, extending from some time in the nomad hunting period, until well into the pastoral, semi-settled stage, or perhaps even into the agricultural.   Later I propose to bridge this gap ; but meanwhile it is enough to say that this is not the sole survival from that age. Although we no longer make offerings of food and weapons in our modern cemeteries, the old fear of the dead man's wrath is yet strong within us. Ghosts are still a very real terror to many people : few could spend a night with unconcern in a haunted house ; and grave-yards are places to be avoided in the dark.   These also are records of that vast period, and each will form the subject of enquiry in due course.

CHAPTER IV.

THE ORIENTATION OF GRAVES.

No reason that is fully satisfying has ever been given for the custom of orienting graves. The explanations of those who practice it carry no conviction : they are no more than wild surmises based on traditions that are faded and illegible. Man is always trying to fit the square peg of belief into the round hole of fact and he fills up the chinks with fancy.

The custom is world wide and very ancient. " In the Predynastic Age in Egypt the corpse was buried lying flexed upon the left side with the head south. . . . About twenty centuries before the Christian era a group of people closely akin to the Predynastic Egyptians came from the south and settled in Nubia. When these people first came north they were in the habit of burying their dead, contracted on the right side, head east. In the second and third Dynasties in Egypt the corpse was buried lying sharply contracted with the head north and the face east. In the eneolithic period the old neolithic rite of inhumation in trench graves still prevailed in many parts of Italy from Brescia to Samnium. The bodies were buried flexed and usually placed upon the left side with the head towards the north-west or north-north-west, and the face was turned in a direction between north and east. In some cases both hands were placed at the head; but most frequently the right hand lies in front of the pelvis, often grasping a dagger." [1].

Similar habits exist in the present day and the explanation of those who practice them is that the dead are placed so to face the Land of Spirits, the Other World. " The Guarayos of South America bury their dead facing to the east whither they are to go. [2] The Samoans and Fijians, agreeing that the land of the departed lies in the far west, bury the corpse lying with the head east and the feet west : the body would but have to rise and walk straight onward to follow its soul home. This idea is stated expressly among the Winnebagos of North America ; they will sometimes bury a dead man sitting up to the breast in a hole in the ground, looking westward : or graves are dug east and

[1] G. Elliott Smith, *Essays Presented to W. Ridgeway*.
[2] Tylor, *Primitive Culture*, vol. ii., p. 72.

west, and the bodies laid in them with the head eastward, with the motive that they may look towards the happy land in the west. The Yumanas of South America bury their dead bent double with faces looking toward the heavenly region of the sunrise, the home of their great good deity, who they trust will take their souls with him to his dwelling. The Guarayos bury the corpses with the heads turned to the east, for it is in the eastern sky that their god Tamoi, the Ancient of Heaven, has his happy hunting-grounds where the dead will meet again. On the other hand the Peruvian custom was to place the dead huddled up in a sitting posture with faces turned to the west. Barbaric Asia may be represented by the modern Ainos of Yesso, burying the dead lying robed in white with the head to the east, ' because that is where the sun rises ' . . . and the Christian usage of digging graves east and west, which prevailed through mediæval times is not yet forgotten."[1]

In this matter of orientation we are of course pursued, as everywhere else in the realms of anthropology, by that bug-bear the solar myth theory. It should have been buried long ago—facing east towards Germany, its spiritual home. A far more interesting theory is that of

[1] Tylor, *Primitive Culture*, vol., ii., pp. 422, 423.

Mr. W. J. Perry who, in a very illuminating essay,[1] shows that in Indonesia the Land of the Dead corresponds with the original home of the race. " In many cases where the dead are supposed to return to the land of the forefathers, the body is placed in a position that is in a direct relation to the direction in which the ghost has to travel. The Badoej inter their dead in an east-west position, with the head at the west end ; the body lies on the right side, so that it is thus facing the south, the direction of the land of the dead. The Panjin cremate their dead in a sitting position facing the east, and the Savoe folk inter their dead in a sitting position facing the west. The dead are thus not only supposed to go in a certain direction, but they are so placed that their attitude is in a definite relation to this direction."

Mr. Perry fails to realise the full significance of his discovery. He shows that the land of the dead is, among the tribes of Indonesia, their land of origin ; that the dead are believed to return there ; and that the bodies are therefore placed facing in that direction. But he does not explain the origin of the belief. How did the idea first arise that the dead return to the home of their ancestors ? *That* he has not attempted to

[1] *Myths of Origin. Folk-Lore.* xxvi., p. 139.

explain, yet it is the problem which lies at the root of the whole matter : it needs to be explained, and I hope to make it clear in due course. For the present we are not concerned with it, but with the fact that bodies are buried lying in a certain direction.

If we rejoin the palæolithic hunter, whom we left sheltered in the grotto at Aurignac waiting for his wounds to heal, we may see him a few days later push down the slab of rock that closed the entrance and emerge, with his weapons in his hands, ready to start on the difficult and dangerous journey home. How did he find the way ? Tradition, in the guise of funeral rites, tells that his companions before consigning him to his resting place instructed him in the direction he would have to take. We gave an example of this in the second chapter when a public address was made to the corpse. Similar customs exist elsewhere, as for example among the Tami, a people of Melanesian stock who inhabit a group of islands off the mainland of New Guinea. When a man is on the point of death the relatives call out, " Miss not the way."[1] But after spending days and nights of pain alone in a lonely grotto, a wounded man might easily forget. Sometimes he might follow the footprints of those who had gone on before, and a record of this survives

in the Welsh belief that it is a sign of good augury
if it rains enough to wet the bier while carrying
it from the house to the church. This appears
to mean enough rain to make the footprints
show, but not enough to wash them away. We
may hazard a guess that the Egyptians painted
signs on the cave walls so that the sick man could
refresh his memory, for they developed this to
a remarkable degree in later times. Another
precaution appears to have been to leave a dog
with the injured man. Certain Esquimaux lay
a dog's head in a child's grave that the soul of
the dog, who is everywhere at home, may guide
the helpless infant to the land of souls. In
accordance with this Captain Scoresby in Jame-
son's Land found a dog's skull in a small grave,
probably a child's. Again, among the Aztecs
one of the principal funeral ceremonies was to
slaughter a techichi, or native dog ; it was burned
or buried with the corpse, with a cotton thread
fastened to its neck.[1]

But dogs are not infallible guides, explanations
may be forgotten, and footprints become
obliterated. Something more was needed by
the wounded man to start him in the right
direction. If he started wrong he might wander

[1] Sir J. G. Frazer, *Belief in Immortality*, vol. i., lecture xiv.,
p. 300. Macmillan 1913.

indefinitely searching for footprints, blazed trees, and the o her indications known to trackers throughout the world—the lingua franca of the wild man. If something more was needed we may feel sure that something more was done. It was done ; and we have records of it, as wide spread as was the need, reaching as far forward into civilization as it extends backwards into savagery, and as simple and obvious in practice as the modern rite that represents it has proved mysterious. If the wounded man was placed lying on his back he had only to sit up in order to face the way he must go, while if placed on his side he was always looking in the right direction.

Orientation in early times had, of course, nothing to do with the points of the compass. Bodies of an early race in Italy are found with the head lying north-west, or north-north west, and we can scarcely credit these people with having learned to divide a circle into eight parts. Men were placed in such a way as to indicate either the general direction of their journey, or that in which they must first set out. As men travelled by day, the sun was no doubt their guide, and instructions probably took much the same form as among travelling folk they do to-day. For example : go towards the rising sun until you come to a river, then follow its bank till you reach a swamp, and so on. In Egypt it was found that the direction of the Nile was the factor governing the orientation of the grave. When the Nile overflowed its banks it must often have been difficult to know which way the current flowed, so the refuge was oriented to make it clear which way was upstream and which way down.

CHAPTER V.

Max Müller defined myth as a disease of
language : I would prefer to call it a lapse of
memory. The events of ancient days are recorded
in tradition, but so greatly have conditions
changed that its meaning is obscure ; and as
each succeeding generation, telling the old
remembered stories to the next, tries to make
plain what is not fully understood, confusion
and misunderstanding are increased, truth is
distorted past recognition, and history becomes
myth. Current beliefs about the Land of the
Dead have arisen in the same way. Unrelated
facts are strung together like different kinds of
beads on one string, and to add to the confusion
people have exercised their ingenuity for countless
years in explaining how they got there. Our
task must be to cut the string and sort the beads
according to their kind.

There is great variety in the descriptions of the
other world : for some it is a pleasant land,

for others the reverse : sometimes it lies beyond
the sea or beneath it, sometimes overhead :
often it is underground ; and not infrequently
it is located somewhere on the surface of the
earth. Almost always it is at a great distance,
though in some few instances, as for example
among the Bretons, the dead men share the
country with the living. It is indeed a tangled
skein that has to be unravelled, " a mighty maze
of works without a plan," as Pope first wrote
the line. The Breton legend will requite a
chapter to itself : stories of the land beneath
the sea will be separated from accounts of voyages
to distant shores ; and the persistent tradition
of an underground world will occupy a section
all alone. But for the present we will restrict
ourselves to the type of story which describes
the Land of the Dead as a distant region of this
world.

In the previous chapter, when considering the
custom of orienting graves, a reference was
made to Mr. Perry's proofs[1] that, in Indonesia,
the Land of the Dead is the country of origin
of the people. A few extracts will indicate his
line of argument.

" An examination of the beliefs of the peoples
inhabiting Indonsia regarding death, reveals the

[1] *Folk-Lore*, xxvi., No. 2, p. 139.

fact that the ghosts of the dead are sometimes supposed to go to a land of the dead situated somewhere on this earth. For example, the Badoej of Bantam place their land of the dead in the south of the Island of Java, at a place called Lemah Bados, "the white spot" : the inhabitants of the Barbar archipelago place their land of the dead west of the group : the Pangin of the Ella district of Borneo believe that the land of the dead is situated to the east of their present habitat : and, in Savoe, an island to the south-west of Timor, the dead are supposed to go to the west. If the traditions of these peoples be examined, it will be found that the direction of the land of the dead in each case is the same as the direction of the land whence they believe themselves to have come. The Badoej came from the south : the people of the Babar archipelago from the west : the Pangin from the east : and the people of Savoe say that their ancestor settled on an island, Randjoewa, situated west of the group." [1] At Bartle Bay in British New Guinea the dead are buried on their sides with their heads pointing in the direction from which the totem clan of the deceased is said to have come originally. [2]

[1] *Folk-Lore*, xxvi., p. 139.
[2] Sir J. G. Frazer, *The Belief in Immortality*, vol. i., lecture ix., p. 208, Macmillan 1913.

'' The Babar people place their dead in canoes.
They place their land of the dead across the
sea, and thus it becomes possible that the canoe
is associated with this fact. A study of the
distributions of the disposal of the dead in canoes
and a belief in a land of the dead or a land of
origin reached by water shows that this surmise
is well founded, and that the two are in correspondence. For example, canoe-coffins are used
by the Galela people of Halmahera, and they
have a tradition that their ancestors came over
the sea from the north-west. Again, the people
of Timorlao place their land of the dead over
the sea whence they have come, and they place
their dead in canoes which shall serve for the
journey back to the land of origin.[1] The next
case is important, for it shows that the use of
a canoe coffin may in some cases have been more
than symbolical. It also shows in yet another
way how close may be the relationship between
the living and the dead. The Olo Ngadjoe of
south-east Borneo believe that the land of the
dead is situated up the river on which they live.
The disposal of the dead has two stages. First,
the body is placed in a canoe-coffin, *raung*, which
is placed in a direction parallel to that of the
river, and is left for some time, generally two

[1] *Folk-Lore*, vol xxvi., No. 2, p. 141.

years, when the second part of the disposal is performed. On the night before the bones are placed in the mausoleum, *sandong*, which is to serve as their final resting place, a litany is chanted by a priest. The theme is a description of the journey of the ghost, guided by the priest, to the land of the dead. It has been thought by many that these descriptive chants are the purely fictitious products of imagination, but information is given by Kruijt which puts quite a different complexion on the matter. Herr F. E. Brackes of Banjermassin has discovered that the Olo Ngadjoe came from Mambaroeh, a district between the upper Kahajan and the Melawi, so that they must have descended the Kahajan on their way to their present home in the south. A place mentioned in the chant as made wholly of gold is a spot actually situated between two bends of the river, called *sating malenak bulan*, " the sating-flower glistening like gold." Further up the river is a spot described in the chant as *baras bulan busong hitan*, " the sand is of gold and the banks of precious stones " : this is the place where gold was formerly washed ; and so on. Further, the boats used in the last part of the journey are much smaller than those used farther down. They are called in the song *banama rohong*, and Kruijt tells us that " this

word rohong is identical with *raung*, the ordinary
word for coffin.   The coffin is thus a canoe."[1]

Mr. Perry contents himself with existing facts
and certain deductions to be drawn from them,
but does not greatly concern himself about
their origin. Accepting without question the
universal fallacy that belief gives rise to custom,
he argues thus : People believe that the souls
of the dead return to the land of their ancestors
so they invented certain funeral rites in
conformity with their belief. For the purpose
for which his article was written the error is of
little moment, for he has arrived, in spite of it,
at results of lasting value : he has provided
another guide by which to trace the footsteps
of migration.   But he leaves unsolved the
problem how men came to hold such ideas.   That
is the purpose of this volume, and the solution
will be found to strengthen, and at the same time
to clarify Mr. Perry's argument.

There is, as I am well aware, a serious break
in the line of my own argument with what looks
very like the river Styx running in between.
The traffic hitherto has been ferried across on
assumptions ; and so it must continue to be for
a little while more. But the gap will be bridged
eventually, and we shall see that what was

[1] *Folk-Lore*, vol. xxvi., p. 142.

mistaken for the river Styx is in fact the
deep waters of Lethe. Meantime I must
crave hospitality for the assertion that what
is now done for the dead was once done for the
living.

Long ages lie between the period we are now
concerned with and the days when the wounded
hunter of the early stone age was hidden in
the grotto at Aurignac. During this vast lapse
of time communities have increased in size,
and advanced in culture. It is no longer a
question of a hunting party, or even of a small
clan, moving from one camping ground to
another because game was getting scarce. We
are dealing now with a state of things not so
very different from what exists to-day : not with
migration, but with emigration ; with communities that have become overgrown, and from
which sections have detached themselves to break
new ground. Early emigrants even to-day
encounter hardships that only the strong can
bear. Canada and the United States both
furnish recent proofs of this. The failures return
whence they came : the strong remain and
found new settlements. That appears to have
been the state of things in Indonesia when the
customs and beliefs described by Mr. Perry
took their rise.

Among the Kachins of Northern Burma it is the custom for the youngest son of a Chief to inherit his father's village. The elder brothers, with a following, break off and found new villages of their own.[1] As a rule they do not venture far, but even so the life in the new settlement is not so easy as in the old. For the ancient Indonesian emigrants the hardships, sufferings, and dangers must have been far greater, and those who could not take their share would be a burden that the community could not carry. The obvious remedy was to send them back. But they must find their own way for no one could be spared to accompany them. All that could be done was to put them in a safe place facing the right direction and provide them with what was necessary for the journey.

That the weak were sent back to their old home is also borne out by customs prevailing among the aborigines of Australia. Among the tribes of Victoria it is the custom to bury a dead man at the spot where he was born. When a black becomes seriously ill he is carried a long distance to the spot where he should die. Dying persons, especially those dying from old age, generally express an earnest desire to be taken

[1] This custom resembles " borough-English " by which estates descended to the youngest son, an institution also existing in Wales. (*The Century Dictionary*.)

to their birthplace, that they may die and be buried there.[1] This recalls the Chinese custom of sending the bodies of their dead back to China for burial. Again, Lieutenant Colonel Collins, who was Governor of New South Wales in the early days of the colony, at the end of the eighteenth century, reports that when natives were questioned as to what became of them after their decease, some answered that they went either on or beyond the great water ; but by far the greater number signified that they went to the clouds. Again, the Narrinyeri tribe of South Australia believed that all the dead went up to the sky and that some of them at least became stars.[2] In this picturesque belief we have an interesting example of the evolution of myth from an ancient custom that had ceased. It appears to recall a time of migration from overseas, perhaps from islands now submerged that once lay off the coast. Charts show that outside a belt of deep water the sea is less than one thousand fathoms deep, while numerous shallows occur nearer to the mainland. All or much of this at one time may have been dry land, just as a rising and submergence of the land has been proved to have occurred in comparatively

[1] Sir J. G. Frazer, *The Belief in Immortality*, vol. i., lecture vii., p. 160, Macmillan 1913.
[2] *Ibid.*, vol. i., lecture vi., p. 133.

recent times in the British Isles. The prevailing winds in that region are north-east and south-west, which would make it easy for a seafaring people to pass from the islands to the mainland and back. With these facts, or rather suppositions, in mind let us consider the superstition once more. The dead—that is, originally, those who were not strong enough to remain with the emigrants, and had to be sent back to their homes—went beyond the great water. They went to the clouds, the sky, and the stars. This is precisely how it would appear to any one standing on the shore and looking out over the sea in the direction they would sail : no land would be visible, but by day they would see the bank of clouds on the horizon, and by night the stars which are the mariners' guide. When, owing to the sinking of the land, all commerce between the two regions ceased it would still be the horizon with its clouds, and by night some guiding stars, that men would point to as the destination of those who used to be sent back—those who were lost to the community, the weak, the sick, and the dying. Taken by itself this is all surmise, but in conjunction with other practices and beliefs, quoted elsewhere in this volume, it attains to some degree of probability.

Similar customs, from northern Europe and Bengal are quoted by Kelly.[1] " Sigmundr carried the body of his beloved son Sinfiötli to the sea shore where a man with a small boat offered it a passage. Sigmundr laid the body in the boat, which had then its full lading ; the unknown boatman pushed off from the shore and floated away with the corpse. . . . In the old French romance of Lancelot du Lac the demoiselle d'Escalot (Tennyson's Lady of Shalott) gives these directions for the disposal of her body after death : ' le pria que son corps fut mis en une nef, richement équipée, que l'on laisseroit aller au gré du vent sans conduite.' " Another example quoted combines an account of the departure by water with the belief in an underground land of the dead. " A Swedish popular legend tells of a golden ship lying underground in Runemad, on board of which Odin conveyed the slain in Bravalla to Valhalla." Finally the older custom merges into the practice of cremation. " The Norse story of the death of Baldr tells how the Æsir raised his funeral pile on board a ship, laid his body on it, and committed the blazing vessel to the waves." Kelly quotes a similar custom from Bengal :

[1] Walter K. Kelly, *Curiosities of Indo-European Tradition and Folk-Lore*, p. 118 (Chapman and Hall, 1863).

" Among the Garrows of Bengal the dead were kept for four days and burnt on a pile of wood in a dingey or small boat."

I will conclude with some examples that deserve further investigation. The following quotation from the *Lapp who cheated Death* was published in the *Manchester Guardian*, April 20th, 1909.[1] " Summer had come. The dwarf birches were in leaf, the arctic brambles in blossom. Svänti, my Lapp host, lay at full length chewing tobacco. . . Such a question as ' Why is snow white ? ' never failed to draw forth some of his legendary lore.

" Snow is white and ice is white because white is the colour of death. Ice and snow come from the home of the dead, the land of darkness, far away in the north. There dwells the Reindeer of Death. When he comes south his sledge is empty, driverless ; when he goes north it is filled with the souls of the dead and the chief among them holds the rein. Sometimes on still winter nights one may hear the click of hoofs though the herd is far off, and no living creature stirs ; then it is that the mother hushes her child and whispers, ' Be still lest the Reindeer of Death should hear you, for he is roaming about seeking souls to fill the empty sledge.' "

[1] Quoted in *Folk-Lore*, vol. xxv., p. 388.

The story concludes : " ' Tell me one thing,'
I begged. ' If the white Reindeer carries off the
dead in its sledge across the snow, what happens
to the souls of those Samelats (*i.e.* Lapps) who
die in summer ? ' Svänti looked at me sideways
with a puckered brow and muttered something
in Lappish. ' It is not lucky to speak so much
of the dead,' he said at last in Norwegian, ' for
we know that the souls of Samelats wander
about during the days of sunshine, waiting until
the sledge comes to fetch them in the dark
months.' "

In this story we have a vivid record of the
old conditions in which the useless members of
the community were sent back to the older
settlement. Sledges being the only means of
transport they could not be sent back when
there was no snow, so they were left to wander
as outlaws on the outskirts of the settlement
until the winter came. One can well imagine
that the emigrants could not afford to support
those who could not take their share of the toil
and hardships. On the other hand, the winter
journey to the older settlement must have been
one that the weak and infirm would gladly evade
if possible ; and it was only by excommunication
and the miseries attendant on it, when even death
on the road would be preferable to the miseries

they were enduring, that they could be induced to depart.

The practice of cremation is a late importation among the Karen. Formerly all were interred and the ghost was supposed to go to the underground. Before interment four bamboo splints are taken and one is thrown towards the west, saying, " That is the east." Another is thrown towards the east, saying, " That is the west." A third is thrown towards the top of the tree, saying, " That is the foot of the tree," and a fourth is thrown downwards, saying, " That is the top of the tree." The source of the stream is then pointed to, saying, " That is the mouth of the stream," and the mouth of the stream is then pointed to, saying, " That is the head of the stream." [1]

This remarkable ceremony is open to two interpretations. It may be, and possibly is, merely a variant of the very wide spread custom of preventing the return of the dead man. With the pretence of instructing him in the way he should take, they reverse everything in order to mislead him. This is perhaps the most natural explanation ; but it is not impossible that the custom records a stage in the migration of the tribe when the direction of the march was altered.

[1] *Folk-Lore*, vol. xxvi., p. 148.

After travelling northwards and upwards into the mountains they turned south and descended to the plains, or *vice versa*. Then the east, which had been on one hand would be on the other, while their movements, which hitherto had been upward, towards the tops of the trees, would be downward towards the foot. Whether this interpretation is correct can only be proved by a detailed investigation of the movements of the particular tribe of Karen among whom the rite exists ; but in Arabia we have an indication of how a similar custom might have arisen among primitive people speaking a primitive tongue. The Arabs migrated from the north, and as they moved southwards the fertile province known as the Yemen, bordering the Red Sea, was on their right. The word Yemen means the right hand side. Now, suppose some Arab tribes had turned back and retraced their steps the Yemen, the right hand side, would have then become their left hand side. It is impossible with our present knowledge, to say whether this did actually occur among the Karen, but the real meaning of a custom is often so disguised that one must be careful not to ignore any side-lights thrown on it

CHAPTER VI.

LOST ATLANTIS.

Mr. Perry's theory has been mentioned that, among the Indonesian races, the land of the dead is the land of origin from which the people migrated. He shows that when a people has migrated by water it is a usual custom to dispose of the dead by placing them in a canoe facing towards the old home. This is a survival from a period of emigration when those who could not take their share of the hardships to which the new colony was subject were sent back to the older settlement, having come in canoes, they returned by canoe. Mr. Perry further points out that the word for a coffin and a canoe are the same in at least one instance, while the ritual of their burial service, which describes the journey to the land of souls, mentions places that can still be recognised lying on the route to the former abode of the people. In this we have an example, with its explanation, of the widely spread belief that the soul must make a journey over water.

A variety of this occurs in Celtic folk-lore. Le
Braz tells us that according to Breton belief it
it is only the troublesome ghosts who will not
leave the living in peace that are ferried to
islands across the sea ; and there is the well-
known story of the village of Tévennec[1] whose
inhabitants are called up in the night to ferry
souls across the sea to the island of the dead.
Here we have no question of a return to the
ancient home of the race : invading German
tribes had conquered that country and there was
no old home to go to ; and, as we shall see,
Breton folk-lore makes little mention of a journey
except for troublesome souls. In the light of
later chapters this variety of the oversea myth
will be explained as a relic of the means taken
by the community to free themselves of the
more turbulent outlaws who persisted in violating
their sentence of banishment.

All these beliefs record an earlier state of life :
they are history in disguise : their meaning has
been indicated in former chapters ; and more
light will be thrown on them as we proceed.
But there is yet another type of myth that tells
of a land beneath the sea—Lost Atlantis, the
Breton City of Is, and all the other tales like
these which are variations of the story of the

[1] Le Braz, *Légende de la Mort* (1912), vol. i., p. 43.

Flood. Sometimes the dwellers in these submerged cities are supposed to be alive, or in a
state of suspended animation, and Breton
fishermen may hear the church bells ringing in
the City of Is. But the commoner belief by
far is that they have been drowned. Although
the living may sometimes be permitted to visit
these abodes beneath the waves, either in dreams,
or by the aid of some supernatural power, there
are, as far as I am aware, no traditions that
they go there when they die. In this respect
myths of the regions of the dead beneath the
sea differ from those underground. This distinction is very important because it indicates that
the submerged cities have no connection with
burial. But even so they must be mentioned
and explained because they clog our argument.

It is usual to treat these stories as fictions
of the imagination, forgetting that even imagination needs facts to work on ; and a fact that
will explain their origin is not far to seek. These
tales, one and all, appear to be based upon the
well established phenomenon of the movement
of the earth's crust. Geike in *The Great Ice Age*
and Lyell in the *Antiquity of Man* give detailed
descriptions of this movement as it affected
western Europe, and the illustrations in these
two books show, not only that the British Isles

were once joined on to the continent, but that
the land extended far west of Scotland, Ireland,
and France. This vast movement occurred
during the human period, and as the land subsided
the sea gradually advanced until the former
habitations of the people were submerged.

Similarly the Andaman Islands are the tops
of a submerged mountain range extending to
the continent of Asia, and the ancient Negritto
race have a tradition of a flood that drowned
all the world except their own few islands. The
inhabitants of Baluchistan point to sea shells
which are now found some five thousand feet
above sea level as a proof of the truth of their
story of the Deluge. Even if these beliefs exist in
regions that have never been submerged in human
times, this only shows that the people carried
the stories with them in their migrations, or
borrowed them from others whose forefathers
had actual experience of them. Regions where
the people once roamed freely in their wanderings
from camp to camp became submerged beneath
the waves. First the valleys and the plains
were flooded, leaving the hills protruding as a
chain of islands; but the land continued still to
sink until in due course of ages the lower eminences
also disappeared. Doubtless father pointed out
to son how in his young days he used to camp

on ground now covered by the sea, while the sight of battered tree stumps beneath the water corroborated his words. Others would repeat tales they had heard in their childhood, how in former times people could walk dry-foot to such or such an island, while now they must use canoes. Each succeeding generation would hand on the tradition after all the land had disappeared from view, and old-wives tales would tell of lands beneath the sea inhabited by people like themselves. Now, as they could see, there was no land left : it was buried beneath the ocean.

Speculation would be rife as to how this happened. The land appears to be motionless, so it was natural to suppose that the water had risen. Then what had made the water rise ? Evidently heavy rain—what else could ? Did they not often see rivers overflow their banks and flood the surrounding country ? So naturally they would assume that the same thing had happened on a larger scale. Everywhere the same cause produced the same result : appearance was taken for reality. Just as the sun was supposed to revolve round the earth, so the sinking of the land was taken for a rising of the water. Thus arose the story of the flood.

No great cataclysm is involved in this explanation. Had there been one it would not have been recorded. Isolated events are soon forgotten : those that burn themselves into the memory of the race are events constantly repeated, or continuously in progress, so that one generation sees with its own eyes, and compares what it sees with what tradition has handed down. It is true that traditions of the Deluge describe it as a sudden calamity that burst suddenly upon the world ; but all traditions have a tendency to dramatic concentration : they concentrate upon one person, place, or time.

These myths, based on traditions of the movement of the earth's crust are not directly connected with burial. I have alluded to them because some writers have confused the issue by including them among myths of which tell of an existence after death on or beneath the land and also because the traditions themselves have become interwoved.

CHAPTER VII.

UNDERGROUND REGIONS OF THE DEAD.

A Karaite writer, Judah Hadasi, who lived in Constantinople in the first half of the twelfth century, tells the following story very briefly in a polemical work composed by him in the year 1148, called *Eshkol Kakofer*, printed in Gozolow (Eupatoria) in 1836.[1] When describing the various miraculous beings created by God he comes to the story of the Pitikos (the Greek name for the dwarfs and pigmies), and he says :

" In a certain country far away, near Kushand Hairlahby, a great lake where aromatic plants and trees are growing, there lives a people known as the Pitikos. Their height is only of two cubits and a half. They are very numerous. They have their kingdoms and their countries. They have their families, and herds of cattle and flocks of sheep, and round the lake there swarm many kinds of birds. Once a year there is a fight between the birds and these Pitikos. The wise

[1] *Folk-Lore*, xxvi., p. 202.

men among the latter know the day in the year when the battle is to take place. Shortly before the day comes they take their families, their cattle, their flocks, and hide them under the ground, and then they arm themselves with swords and lances, with bows and arrows, with spears and clubs, and they prepare for the fight. The sky gets darkened with the multitude of birds that are coming to attack these dwarfs with their claws and beaks. On both sides many are slain before the sun sets. From the day after there is again peace in the land. The survivors bring their women and children, their cattle and their flocks, from the hiding places, and the birds withdraw.

My Somali servant, Muhammad Dolbehanta, told me he had seen in the interior of Somaliland an immense excavation in the earth with a sloping path leading down into it. Here, he said, the people who inhabited the country before the Somalis conquered it, used to take refuge when attacked, driving their cattle with them.

Mr. R. R. Marett describes in detail the enormous cave of Niaux, near Tarascon in the Little Pyrenees, with its difficult, low, and narrow passages ; its cathedral-like interior three quarters of a mile from the entrance ; its lake protecting recesses even more remote ; and the paintings

on the walls made by men of the pleistocene age.
There are some nineteen painted caves known in
France, and the discoveries in Spain, which every
day increase, bring up the total of such caves
and rock-shelters to at least fifty, besides
innumerable others without paintings.[1]   The
catecombs in Paris and Malta, and similar
excavations explored in Italy,[2] are a later
development of the underground dwelling ; while
in a manuscript by Catari the remarkable statement is made that no judgment can be formed
of the size of the ruined city Tiahuanacu because
nearly all was built underground.[3]

It is not necessary to dwell at length upon the
well established fact that many races in a certain
stage of progress used caves and subterranean
hollows as their normal dwelling places.   The
interesting point for us is that they came in later
times to be regarded as the homes of the dead.
The Algonquin Indian folk-tale of the Red Swan
tells how a hunter, Ojibwa, comes to an opening
in the earth into which he descends and arrives
at the abode of departed spirits.[4]   The Aztecs
believed in a subterranean land of the dead.[5]

[1] *The Threshold of Religion*, R. R. Marett.
[2] *The Contemporary Review*, p. 203. February 1917.
[3] Sir Clements R. Markham, *The Incas of Peru*, chap. ii.
(Smith Elder, 1910).
[4] Tylor, *Primitive Culture*, vol. i., p. 346.
[5] *Ditto*, vol. i., p. 349.

In Brittany rocky clefts are believed to be the entrance to the world of the dead, like the cave of Lough Dearg.[1] In Scandinavia the dead were associated with female spirits or *fylgjur* living in hollow hills.[2] Amenti of the ancient Egyptians combines the idea of an under-world and the west. While Sheol of the Israelites lay deep below the earth.

It has been shown in an earlier chapter that the home of the dead is often intimately connected with the land of origin, that is, the district from which the ancestors of the people emigrated. Now, however, the connection appears to be not with the land from which they came, but with the dwellings in which they lived. The Zulus, for example, call their ancestors ' Abapansi,' the " people underground."[3] In South America, Brazilian souls travel down to the world below in the west, and Patagonian souls will depart to enjoy eternal drunkenness in the caves of their ancestral deities.[4] In North America, the Tacullis held that the soul goes after death into the bowels of the earth, whence it can come back in human shape to visit friends.[5]

[1] MacCulloch, *Religion of the Ancient Celts*, p. 344.
[2] *Folk-Lore*, xvii., p. 398.
[3] Tylor, *Primitive Culture*, vol. ii.. p. 66.
[4] *Ditto*, vol. ii., p. 66.
[5] *Ditto*, vol. ii., p. 66.

The fact that the ancestors of living races dwelt in caves, or underground, is often recorded in tradition :—

" Some of the clans of the Old Kuki of Manipur believe that their ancestors came out of the ground.[1]   The Purum clan claim descent from Tonring and Tonshu, who issued out of the ground. These peoples inter their dead as do the inhabitants of Keisar, whose first ancestor sprouted out of Mount Wahkuleren. In Beloe the first ancestress of the people of Fialarang came out of Mount Lekaan, and they also practise interment. Thus an origin from the ground is accompanied by a return to the ground.[2]

" When the dead are interred it is believed that the ghost goes into the underground land of the dead. The Batak of Similoengoen inter their dead, and the land of the dead is situated in the bowels of the earth ; it is a land exactly like this and is situated directly underneath the place which the Batak inhabit. In south-west Timor, where the dead are interred, earthquakes are supposed to be due to the efforts of the dead imprisoned beneath to break out from their underground land. Among the Karen, formerly, all the dead were interred and the ghost was

[1] Among the Papuans the same idea is current, see p. 61 *infra*.
[2] *Folk-Lore*, xxvi., p. 147.

supposed to go to the underground land of the dead."[1]

" Some of the Old Kuki clans of Manipur claim that their ancestors came out of the underground world by means of a cave. The Lamgang say that on the Kangmang Hill, far away to the south there is a cave, and their ancestors, a man and a woman, came out of it. The Patalima of Seran also have a tradition that their ancestors came out of a cave.[2] The Kabui Naga believe that the dead go into the underground world : one mode of disposing of the dead among them is that in which an excavation in the side of a hill is made in which the body is placed, and the opening filled up with stones. The Bunjogee and Pankho claim that their ancestors came out of a cave, and say that " the cave whence man first emerged is in the Lhoosai country close to Vanhuilen. They inter their dead. About their future home they are most expliclt. After death they believe that the deceased go into the large hill whence man first emerged : this they say is the land of the dead."[3]

Speaking of the Celtic gods, MacCulloch says : " Dispater dwelt underground. Some were connected with mounds and hills, or were supposed

[1] *Folk-Lore*, xxvi., p. 148.
[2] See also the Papuan legend quoted in chap. viii., *infra*.
[3] *Folk-Lore*, xxvi., p. 149.

to have taken up their abode in them. . . . In Celtic belief men were not so much created by gods as descended from them. ' All the Gauls assert that they are descended from Dispater, and this, they say, has been handed down to them by the Druids.' (Cæsar, vol. vi., 18). Dispater was a Celtic underworld god, and the statement probably pre-supposes a myth, like that found among many primitive peoples, telling how men once lived underground and thence came to the surface of the earth. . . . Thither the dead returned to him who was ancestor of the living.''[1]

In Hispaniola according to legend men came out of caves : the Incas had traditions of men dwelling in caves like wild beasts : New Zealanders tell how Mani cannot find the cave of the west wind to roll a stone against its mouth.

The Baperi of South Africa will venture to creep a little way into their cavern of Marimatlé, whence men and animals came forth into the world, and whither souls return at death. In Mexico the cavern of Chalchatongo led to the plains of paradise, and the Aztec name of Mictlan, ' Land of the Dead,' now Mitla, keeps up the remembrance of another subterranean

[1] MacCulloch, *Religion of the Ancient Celts.*

temple which opened the way to the sojourn of the blessed. North German peasants still remember on the banks of the swampy Drömling the place of access to departed souls. By Lough Derg is the cavern entrance of St. Patrick's Purgatory leading to the awful world below. In the great Finnish epic, Kalewala, the land of the dead is " the underworld Manala." [1]

When a Samoan Islander dies, the host of spirits that surround the house, waiting to convey his soul away, set out with him, crossing the land and swimming the sea, to the entrance of the spirit-world. This is at the western-most point of the westernmost island, Savaii, and there one may see the two circular holes or basins where the souls descend, chiefs by the bigger and plebeians by the smaller, into the regions of the underworld. There below is a heaven, earth, and sea, and people with real bodies, planting, fishing, and cooking. . . . . During the hours of darkness they come up to revisit their former abodes, retiring at dawn to the bush or to the lower regions." [2]

I will conclude with the New Zealand folk tale of Mani, which though twisted into a solar myth by imaginative anthropologists, bears its

---

[1] Tylor, *Primitive Culture*, vol. ii., p. 45.
[2] Tylor, *Primitive Culture*, vol. ii., p. 66

true meaning on the face of it. "One night, when Taranga came home, she found little Mani with his brothers, and when she knew her last-born, the child of her old age, she took him to sleep with her, as she had been used to take the other Manis his brothers before they were grown up. But the little Mani grew vexed and suspicious when he found that every morning his mother rose at dawn and disappeared from the house in a moment, not to return till nightfall. So one night he crept out and stopped every crevice in the wooden window and the doorway, that the day might not shine into the house ; then broke the faint light of early dawn, and then the sun rose and mounted into the heavens, but Taranga slept on, for she knew not it was broad day outside. At last she sprang up, pulled out the stopping of the chinks, and fled in dismay. Then Mani saw her plunge into a hole in the ground and disappear, and thus he found the deep cavern by which his mother went down below the earth as each night departed."[1]

Another tale relates how "The Old Mani lay by his fire in the dead-land of Bulotu, when his grandson Mani came down by the cavern entrance and carried off the fire."[2]

[1] *Idem.* vol. i., p. 343.
[2] *Idem.*, vol. i., p. 364.

CHAPTER VIII.

DWELLINGS AND GRAVES.

Tylor points out that the doctrine of a land of souls on earth belongs widely and deeply to savage culture, but dwindles in the barbaric stage, and survives but feebly into the mediæval ; while the doctrine of a subterranean Hades holds as large a place as this in savage belief, and has held it firmly along the course of higher religions. [1] This appears to indicate that the conditions that gave rise to the former belief belong to a stage of culture far earlier than those on which the subterranean Hades is based. This may well be so. As has been shown, the doctrine of a land of souls on earth had its origin in very early times : first there was the wounded hunter of Aurignac, and later came the stage when emigrants who could not withstand the hardships in new settlements were sent back to their original home. The former belongs certainly to the hunting stage : the latter perhaps to the pastoral. It is not possible to define the stages with accuracy, for they merge into one another.

[1] Tylor, *Primitive Culture*, vol. ii., p. 74.

The agricultural stage of culture, however, brings in a very different state of things. The same area of country will then provide subsistence for a far larger population, and when the ground under cultivation becomes barren for want of manure, the community need not move far in search of new ground. Similarly when the population grows so large that the fields must be extended to an inconvenient distance from their village it is easy to move into the next valley and start afresh. The road there is well known, all the preliminary work of clearing the forest can be done before the move commences, and there will be continual communication between the old and new settlements.

There appear to be indications that in Europe the population outgrew its accommodation every second generation, for there are in Folk-lore frequent references to the " seventh child of a seventh child." Seven, no doubt, meant any large number, as for example when the Jews asked whether one should forgive a brother " unto seven times," restricting the word to its later and stricter significance : and the reply was " unto seventy times seven " thus restoring the original meaning of a vast number.

The new conditions resulting from a more assured food supply, a larger population more evenly distributed, and the mutual assistance and support thus secured, made the eviction of the *bouches inutiles* less necessary. But a more powerful factor still came into play. With the other advances in material culture came an improvement in the dwellings of the people. As long as constant movement is necessary much time and labour will not be spent on dwellings which are soon to be vacated : but when a man spends all his life in one place there is every inducement to improve it. Agricultural life, with its long periods of leisure also affords the opportunity. It is the first period in the history of man in which great progress was made, though not to be compared to that of the modern mechanical age when the accumulation of capital has relieved a large proportion of the population of earning their bread by physical toil. It was in a more or less stationary existence, whether pastoral or agricultural, or in an intermediate stage, that the improvement of dwellings must have occurred.

We have seen in the last chapter the evidence of the extensive use of natural caves. These, however, were not always to be found, and, acting as man has always acted, his first step appears to have been to imitate them. Hitherto he had lived underground, so he continued to do so, digging an artificial cavern for himself and his belongings.

In the Irish *Story of Deirdre* we are told that "Colum Cruiteir got three men, and he took them to a large mountain, distant and far from reach. . . . He caused there a hillock, round and green, to be dug out of the middle, and the hole thus made to be covered carefully over so that a little company could dwell there together. . . and placed with them food for a year and a day."[1]

A modern example is described in Mr. Savage Landor's *Across Coveted Lands*. He says, " I was much interested in some curious circular and quadrangular pits only a few yards from where we stopped, which were used as shelters for men and sheep, but were now deserted. They were from four to six feet deep below the surface of the ground, and from ten to thirty feet in diameter (when circular), a section being partitioned for sheep. . . . In the part reserved for human beings there was a circular fireplace of stones, and some holes in the earth at the sides for storing foodstuff. . . . The difference in temperature between the interior of these pits and the open ground was extraordinary. They were comfortably warm, even when it

[1] *Celtic Magazine*, December, 1887, p. 71.

was uncomfortably cold as one peeped out of them."

Miss J. E. Harrison in an article on Kyllene's hill-cave gives a number of descriptions, gathered from classical and other sources, of underground dwellings. "This combination of hill and cave recalls immediately a class of vases which have long puzzled archæologists. The design shows Satyrs, etc., leaping and kicking round a hillock or artificial mound. In answer to their summons a figure rises up from the cave inside the mound."[1]

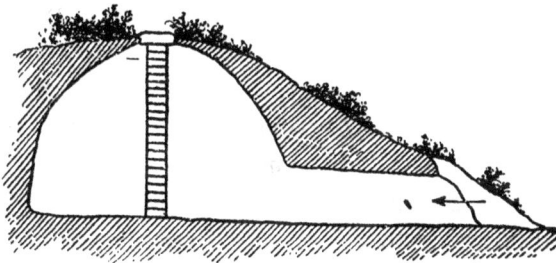

The illustration taken from her essay, shows the cavern closed at the top by a stone, with a ladder leading down into it, while the arrow indicates the entrance for animals. Incidentally it illustrates the story, told to Colonel Shakespear by the Chawte (a Kuki clan of Manipur), of the peopling of the world out of a hole in the ground,

[1] *Essays Presented to Ridgeway*, pp. 138, *et seq.*

when they added the graphic touch that an inquisitive monkey lifted up a stone which lay on the opening, and thus allowed their ancestors to escape.[1]   A similar legend exists among the Papuans.   " According to their belief the land was first covered with scrub but inhabited by man.   Then a great lizard came and scratched a hole in the earth.   Then a dog came and made the hole deeper, then a pig which made it deeper still ; and out of this rose five beautiful maidens who founded five villages."[2]   This appears to indicate that primitive man made use of existing caves and burrows, enlarging them and adapting them to his own requirements, perhaps after driving out or killing their animal occupants.

The custom was not confined to the Phrygians. Xenephon tells us of similar hill-cave dwellings among the Armenians, and he adds important particulars as to the modes of entrance.   " The dwellings were underground, the mouth like a well and wide below.   The entrance for beasts was quarried, but men descended by a ladder. In these dwellings were goats, sheep, oxen, birds, and the offspring of these.   All these cattle being reared on forage within the house."[3]   These

---

[1] *Folk-Lore*, **xxvi.**, p. 149.
[2] Colonel Kenneth Mackay, *Across Papua*, p. 70 (Witherby, 190).
[3] *Essays Presented to Ridgeway*, p. 138.

underground dwellings, as Tacitus notes among the Germans, were the safest and most salubrious of granaries.[1]

" The Greeks who went to help Cyrus against Artaxerxes were retreating through Armenia when they were overtaken by a terrible snowstorm. A whirlwind of hail blew in their faces ; their bodies were stiff with ice ; their beasts of burden fell dead about them ; they themselves must have perished, when happily they came on a village of these hill-cave dwellings, ' these had passages for the cattle dug through the earth, but the people went down by ladders underground, and for the flocks there was hay and for men great abundance of all things needful for life.' Gradually, it would seem, the underground hut ventured to emerge to the upper air. The shape long remained round, that being the simplest form for a structure made of earth or clay or twisted boughs. The square form, so much more handy for the divided dwelling, needed a knowledge of post architecture. Long after man had learned to build solid houses above ground, underground houses went on as ' treasuries ' for all manner of stores and especially for grain."[2]

[1] *Essays Presented to Ridgeway*, p. 140.
[2] Ditto, p. 141.

Reminiscences of these underground dwellings, with their entrance above, recur in various beliefs and customs. " The Roman Orcus was in the bowels of the earth, and when the *lapis manalis*, the stone that closed the mouth of the world below, was moved away on certain solemn days, the ghosts of the dead came up to the world above and partook of the, offerings of their friends."[1] The Chinese make a hole in the roof of their houses to let out the soul at death.[2] The Iroquois in old times used to leave an opening in the grave for the lingering soul to visit its body.[4] In the Congo district, the custom has been described of making a channel into the tomb to the head or mouth of the corpse, whereby to send down offerings of food and drink."[3] While the custom of opening a window for the departing soul when it quits the body is to this day a very familiar superstition in France, Germany, and England.

When people began to live in the hut above the hillock, and the cave below was used as a storehouse, because it was safer—and probably, for the same reason, as a refuge in time of danger —it seems to have served also as a shelter for the sick and injured. So when customs changed

---

[1] *Essays Presented to Ridgeway*, p. 141.
[2] Tylor, *Primitive Culture*, vol. ii., p. 67.
[3] *Ibid.*, vol. i., pp. 453, 454.
[4] *Ibid.*, vol. ii., p. 31.

it developed into a grave, and of this we find
many records still surviving. Some mountain
tribes of New Guinea bury their dead beneath
their huts.[1] Similarly it is recorded that in
in Nijne Kolymsk, in North East Siberia, during
an epidemic of small-pox there were not enough
of graves to contain all the corpses, and many
were buried in the store-holes under the huts.[2]
This appears to be a reversion under pressure
of difficult conditions, to an older custom. On
the island of Tumleo at Berlin Harbour in German
New Guinea the dead are placed in a wooden
coffin and buried in a grave which is dug either
in the house or close by it. When the grave is
dug outside the house, a small hut is erected over
it, and a fire is kept burning over it until the ghost
is supposed to have reached Sisano, which is a
place on the mainland a good many miles to the
north of Tumleo.[3]

Researches in Egypt have brought to light
a most instructive series of examples ranging
from the most primitive shelter barely large
enough to contain one man, through the period
when it became a many chambered subterranean
dwelling, and down to the time when the purpose

[1] Colonel K. Mackay, *Across Papua*, chap. x., p. 142
(Witherby, 1909).
[2] Shklovski, *In Far N.E. Siberia*, pp. 27, 108 (Macmillan,
1916).

of it had been forgotten and the pyramids were built to contain one dead man's body. The following extracts are taken from Mr. G. Elliott-Smith's article " Tomb-Evolution in Egypt,"[1] and though he accepts the usual doctrine that graves were always graves, the original intention that they were refuges for the living is not totally obscured. He speaks of " the ever present idea of the grave as a dwelling for the deceased " and " whereas the more ancient coffin and *mastaba* simulated the simple prehistoric hut, the later (Third Dynasty) application of the house-idea to the subterranean tomb made of it a contemporary house."

" In the Predynastic Age in Egypt the corpse was buried lying flexed upon the left side, with the head south : it was protected from contact with the soil by linen, mats, or skins, or in the larger tombs by a palisade of sticks or a wooden frame in the grave. The small graves were shallow pits of an oval or nearly round form ; the larger graves were deeper rectangular pits, roofed with branches of trees."

Speaking of somewhat similar graves in Italy, when the right hand of the corpse was often found grasping a dagger, he says " There are indications that sometimes the graves were

[1] *Essays Presented to Ridgeway.*

roofed with wood." If these graves are not of comparatively recent date, that is, if they were refuges and not graves, we may hazard the guess that they were always roofed though only sometimes indications remain.

Similar graves are made by the Tamos of Astrolabe Harbour in German New Guinea who bury the dead in a grave about three feet deep and four feet long dug inside the house. If the corpse is too long for the grave the legs are doubled up and trampled in. The body is shrouded in mats or leaves, and the grave is covered with wood so that the mould which is heaped on the top may not press on the body.[1]

Mr. Elliott-Smith goes on to say, " At the end of the Predynastic period the practice was introduced of lining the grave with brickwork to prevent the sand falling in and also to support a roof of branches, logs with layers of bricks upon them, or later, corbel vaults, which were certainly invented about this time in Egypt." " In Nubia the graves were cut, not in loose sand as in Egypt, but in hard mud. Wood, rare enough in Egypt,[2] could be obtained in

---

[1] Sir J. G. Frazer, *Belief in Immortality*, vol. i., p. 234 (Macmillam, 1913).

[2] " Wood was by no means so rare in early times as it is now in Egypt. Floyer has shown how much the desert has been stripped by the introduction of the tree-feeding camel. We see in the royal tombs of the first dynasty a large use of

Nubia much less often, so slabs of stone were used for roofing graves. When the corbel-vault was invented in Egypt the Nubians imitated it by cutting beehive-shaped graves in the mud.[1] The advantage of this type was that the hole to be closed was smaller, and slabs of stone of sufficient size were more easily obtained.

" As the material prosperity of Egypt increased, it found expression in an aggrandisement of the tomb and in all the provisions made for the welfare of the corpse. . . . In Protodynastic times, as the grave increased in size, logs of wood were used for roofing it, and layers of mud-brick were put upon the logs further to protect the burial from damage or desecration. But the time arose when the tombs of the wealthy became so large . . . that it became necessary to erect walls to break up the extent of the spaces to be spanned by the roofing beams. Hence the grave became converted into a suite of rooms one of which was occupied by the

wood. The funeral chamber sunk in the ground was entirely built of massive beams and planks. The area of this room was 900 feet square in the largest tomb, varying down to 300 in the lesser. The framing of the floor, the supports, and the roof beams were about 10 by 7 inches in section, and up to 21 feet in length. The planking of the floor still remains 2 to 2½ inches thick ; and probably that of the roof was equal to it, as it has to bear about three feet of sand over it." Flinders Petrie, *The Arts and Crafts of Ancient Egypt*, chap. xiii. (Foulis, 1909).

The relative antiquity appears open to question.

corpse and the others became mere magazines for the multitude of pots.   The grave also became so deep that an incline or a flight of steps had to be made, not only for the workmen engaged in the construction, but also for those who entered the tomb at the burial ceremony." [1]

It is not necessary to follow him in tracing the later development of Egyptian tombs, for before they began to develop to any great extent it is probable the people had long forgotten that they had once been refuges and dwellings for the living.

[1] But see p. 61 where it is shown that the sloping side-entrance was for the passage of flocks and herds.

CHAPTER IX.

THE BRETON LAND OF THE DEAD.

In an earlier chapter I discussed certain beliefs
and customs which were found to imply that the
land of the dead was the land of origin. It was
a distant land involving a troublesome journey
to reach it, though its direction was well known.
According to my interpretation these customs
and beliefs record a period of emigration when
those who could not endure the hardships that
surrounded enterprising colonists were sent back
to the older settlement where life was easier.
This was an adaptation, in a much later period,
of the ancient custom of putting a wounded man
in safety until sufficiently recovered to rejoin
his companions. In neither instance could
primitive communities endure the burden of
maintaining those who were not fit to take
their share of the difficulties and dangers that
surrounded them. Both customs imply movement, either of nomads or of emigrants : in the
older, a man's companions left him : in the
more recent, he left them.

We are now about to consider a different class of facts in which there is no separation, no journey, but the dead continue to share the land with the living. In one respect only do these beliefs resemble the others, and that is that the dead inhabit the surface of the earth. Brittany is the home of this belief though it still survives, in a less degree, in Scotland, Ireland, and Wales. In the British Isles, however, it appears to have become confused with traditions of the aboriginal races with whom the Celtic invaders inter-mingled. It is true that in other lands we also find remnants lingering in isolated superstitions, but in Brittany almost alone it still survives in comparative purity, forming a large part of the mental equipment of the people.

Among the Bretons, only the dead who are unbearably troublesome to the living are sent on a journey to the other world, the others continue to dwell among the living. "On a pu dire," says Le Braz, "On a pu dire de la Bretagne qu'elle était avant toute chose le pays de la mort. . . . Pas plus que le Gaulois du temps de Lucain ou les Gaels de la vieille Irlande, les Bretons ne relèguent les morts dans une patrie distincte de celle des vivants." To Yeun Elez are sent only restless and dangerous souls, those that cannot be kept quiet anywhere but

there; while the rock of Tévennec and the
other maritime regions of the dead are the
dwellings only of the restless souls of men who
are lost at sea. " Le surplus—c'est-à-dire
l'immense majorité des morts—on ne se les
représente accomplissant ces lointaines équipées
funèbres. Il semble qu'en entrant dans la tombe,
ils entrent du même coup dans l'autre vie. Ils
revivent donc, en définitive, aux lieux mêmes
ou ils ont toujours vécu. Le séjour des morts
se confond avec celui des vivants. Il n'est
plus ici ou là, dans tel canton terrestre ou dans
tel îlot marin : il est partout : il s'étend aussi
loin que s'étend la Bretagne, et c'est le pays
breton tout entier qui devient à la lettre le 'pays
des morts.' " [1]

The dead remain in Brittany ; if one may say
so, they live in Brittany, and by night they own
the country. For the most part they are
feared and propitiated by the living who hardly
venture unaccompanied to stir abroad during
the hours of darkness. Breton folk-lore does
not regard the dead as having ceased to live,
but rather as people who for some mysterious
reason are obliged to dwell apart while yet retaining an affection for their home and friends—a
sentiment that often is requited in spite of the

[1] Le Braz, *Legende de la mort*, vol. i., p. 49.

dread that they inspire. The popular stories collected by Le Braz furnish a most detailed account of the ' life ' of the dead. So far from being disembodied spirits they suffer from cold, and thirst, and hunger, and it is believed that they may even be wounded, for Le Braz says : " C'est une croyance très repandu qu'on pent blesser l'âme." They labour in the fields, watch over the welfare of friends and relations, revenge themselves on those who have done them wrong, and even repay debts left undischarged. Each retains the characteristics that distinguished him in life, though he may suffer remorse for evil he has done. In short, if it were not for the use of the words ' dead ' and ' soul ' one would assume without hesitation that persons were referred to who, in compliance with some custom, are out-laws from the community.

And this, originally, I take to have been the fact. Why the word ' dead " (trépassé) [1] was applied to them I shall endeavour later on to show. Meantime there is another interesting problem to be solved. Why, in Brittany almost alone, have the dead to make no journey ? Why only here do they continue to live with the living ?

---

[1] The original meaning of *trepassé* was " to pass beyond."
See p. 10!.

Whatever may have been the origin of the Celtic speaking people it appears to be certain that at one time they inhabited central Europe whence they were expelled by German or Teutonic tribes. Always retiring before superiority of numbers, culture, or organization, they spread east, and west, and south, mingling with the people into whose territories they were driven, and thus produced the very varied Celtic types that now exist.

During this period of wandering there must have been many whose presence was not merely a burden but a danger to the rest ; the old and infirm, the sick and injured, not to mention the lazy and troublesome. Among the Indonesian tribes, as we have seen, these were sent back to the older settlement, the home of their fathers. But the movement of the Celtic people was not emigration : it was an exodus. They were driven from their homes by the pressure of invading foes who occupied the country they had left. So for the aged and infirm, the sick and injured, there was no question of a journey home : there was no home to go to. Yet custom and hard necessity required their expulsion from the tribe. Their condition must have been pitiable in the extreme. Like the civil population of a beleaguered fortress, thrust out by the garrison and driven back by the foe, they wandered homeless and starving between two armies.

This explains why in Breton folk-lore there is no journey home for the dead. Yet the explanation is not complete ; for customs, as we know outlive their usefulness, and beliefs die hard. The story of the Celtic exodus is modern history, perhaps as recent as three thousand years ago. Before that time there must have been a period of growth when each small community threw off its surplus population to found new settlements. These must have found their feebler members a hindrance to their welfare ; and, as was done by other races, it seems at least possible that they sent them back to their old home. If, then, in other parts of the world we find records of this early stage in funeral customs and in beliefs about the dead, how is it that none survive in Brittany ?

We may, perhaps, be crediting the early Celts with a kindliness of disposition they did not possess. It is possible that they were more brutal in their methods than other races, and cast out their useless members without caring what became of them. But we have no reason to assume this : indeed, their customs of providing for the comfort of the dead have quite a contrary aspect.

Even if the Celtic people in an earlier stage had methods similar to those of other people for disposing of their useless members, there is a good reason why they should not have survived in custom and belief. This will be more easily made clear if we contrast the Indonesians with the Celts. Among both it is assumed that the custom of getting rid of those who were a burden to them existed during the period of voluntary emigration. The practice of putting a man in a canoe or in a temporary shelter outside the village, with food and weapons for his return journey, was in no sense a ceremony. It was a sensible and practical way of getting rid of him. So was the precaution of placing him facing towards the right direction. But in course of time the Indonesians ceased to find it necessary to send away their feeble members, so the custom fell into disuse. But, for reasons which will be explained later, similar means were adopted of disposing of the dead. So certain of the ancient customs continued to survive as funeral rites, while tradition retained imperfectly the reason for it—a journey.

Among the Celts, however, a sudden change made the practice useless. They were driven out by enemies who occupied their country. But stern necessity still required that a useless member of the community should be turned out, so he *was* turned out. He became an outlaw living as best he could in the forest on the outskirts of the settlement. He could not return to the older settlement because it was occupied by the enemy : so there was no journey for him to make. When at last after perhaps many hundred years the Bretons, like the Indonesians, ceased to find the old and sick an intolerable burden, and certain of these ancient customs were transferred to the dead, tradition had no tale to tell about a journey ; but, instead, it told of the dead as surrounding the habitations of the living.

Note.—To simplify the argument I have omitted the few, and not over clear indications of a time when there was a journey. Le Braz mentions the belief that the dead remain near the living in a state of suffering and then vanish. Also that they look forward to the time of their departure. The superstition about the death-carts driven by the last man who dies, may have the same implication. This superstition is found also in Lancashire and Lincolnshire. (*Folk-Lore*, vol. **xxv.**, p. 388).

CHAPTER X

I have tried to show that funeral rites, and all beliefs concurrent with them bear the strong impress that, in some way which is far from clear, which even those who practise and believe them do not understand, they one and all are intimately connected with a living person. I have insisted that these beliefs and rites are the voice of tradition, speaking in a strange, forgotten tongue, telling how in " old unhappy far-off times " men treated those who were a burden to them. These ancestral voices, mumbling and indistinct with age, are striving to utter things we will not hear. We persist in misunderstanding, and when we can distort their meaning in no other way, we attribute them to the misguided fancy of imaginary ' myth-makers,' to the mental childishness of prehistoric men, to anything indeed of which we are entirely ignorant. Somehow, anyhow, they must be forced to tally with our own ideas.

It is we modern men, barbarian and civilized alike, who are the myth-makers, not those of ancient times. Savages can plead extenuating circumstances; for as Lowell says, "The human mind, when it sails by dead reckoning, without the possibility of a fresh observation, perhaps without the instruments necessary to take one, will sometimes bring up in very strange latitudes." But we can offer no excuse. Travel, history and archæology have provided us with a vast accumulation of facts; yet we accept the conclusions of the savage for no reason but that occasionally they resemble more or less our own. Then, in our turn, we have started on a voyage of discovery and brought up sometimes in very strange latitudes, where solar-myths and other wondrous creations roam about the land unchecked. There is nothing for it but to go back and start afresh.

Hitherto in my argument there has been a very noticeable break. I have claimed that modern burial rites are relics of ancient methods for the protection or disposal of the living; but so far I have not yet shown how the change occurred. At first sight it seems incredible that such a thing could happen. The mystery lies not so much in the change itself, not, that is, in doing for the dead what formerly was done for the living, but in the universal acceptance of the idea that these actions are in some way beneficial to the dead.   It seems, if true, only to be explained by some great mental cataclysm that left the ancient customs undisturbed while obliterating all knowledge of their purpose.   Yet this mighty revolution was brought about by the mere lapse of time, and a progress, imperceptibly slow, in material culture.

It has been shown already how strongly graves resemble primitive dwellings ; also how from taking shelter in caves and fissures, which doubtless they extended and improved, men learned in time to make them artifically by digging into natural hillocks or using the excavated earth to form a mound over the well-like dwelling.   It has been mentioned, too, how the dwelling gradually ventured to emerge above the surface—probably, at first, no more than a slight and temporary shelter—while the property was kept below where the people also retired for protection when danger threatened.   This stage has left its traces even till to-day.   In India the people bury their money beneath the floor of their houses : banks in Europe keep their treasure in cellars : we all do the same with our coal and wine : and, except in the most recently designed hotels, our cooking still is done beneath the ground. In France even the language bears testimony, the French for cellar being *cave*.

We see then that the safety place was underground long after men had learned to live upon the surface, and it was there that the feeble, who were unable to protect themselves, would naturally be placed. These facts, however, do not show how the dead came to be treated as though alive. I have recapitulated them because they bear upon the explanation I am now about to offer.

In the course of ages communities increased, the food supply became more assured, and migration less frequent, dwellings were improved, villages fortified, and dangerous animals exterminated in the settled districts. The old, the sick, the injured and infirm were no longer an insupportable burden to their companions. In these easier conditions they were even useful, they could look after the home, tend sheep or cattle grazing near, collect fuel, prepare the food, and do much other light work that the hardier members were too tired to do after the day's work. The knowledge and experience, that only comes with age, was also useful to the community. This is recorded among the Bouriats who used to put old people to death by making them swallow a long ribbon of fat which choked

them. Legend says it was discontinued because
it was found that the old people gave good
advice.[1] It became not only unnecessary but
unwise to drive them out, or send them back
to the parent settlement as long as they were
any use at all. And as conditions still continued
to improve it became at last unnecessary to send
them away at all. But those who were about
to die continued to be put away according to
ancient custom. The refuges had now become
a place to die in : but as the man was not dead
he still required the same provision to be made
as in former times was provided for the journey.
Professor Fraser quotes an Indian custom where
those upon the point of death are taken out of
bed at the last moment and placed on the bare
earth. This seems to be a relic of the transfer
from the dwelling to the place to die in. Among
the Jains of Bengal it is done in a more realistic
and indeed brutal fashion, for the dying man
is thrown from his bed and dragged along the
ground. Le Braz quotes a similar Breton
custom : " Lorsqu'un moribond a trop de mal
à trepasser, il y a un moyen infaillible d'abréger
son agonie : c'est de le descendre de son lit et
de lui faire poser ses pieds nus sur le sol nu."[2]

---

[1] Shklovsky, *In Far N.-E. Siberia*, p. 243 (Macmillan, 1916).
[2] *Legende de la Mort*, vol. i., p. 84.

Last of all it was not until the man was dead that his body was removed, and the shelter then became a grave, not a place to die in, but a place for the dead. Still tradition spoke darkly of a journey, and custom still required provision to be made for it. " What journey ? " asked future generations. And tradition answered : " The journey that the dead man has to make."

The error was due not only to the survival of the custom : tradition made things worse by using the old words. Nothing is so insidiously misleading as the magic immanent in words. Words have often a magnetic pole that deflects our thoughts from truth : their value is always changing : they mean different things to different men, and are dowered almost with eternal life. Outwardly they remain the same : inwardly they are different. The voice is the voice of Jacob, but the hands are the hands of Esau. It is impossible to realise all that a word implied to those who heard it even a few centuries ago. *Sacre* in French can stand either for ' holy ' or for ' damned,' and Mr. Marett has suggested that the Latin *sacer* merely meant *tabu*.[1] *Trépasser* in its wider sense meant to pass beyond, its restricted meaning now is ' to die.' *Avaler*, from which the Arthurian Vale of Avalon is

[1] *Threshold of Religion*, p. 110.

probably derived, originally was equivalent to
'*faire descendre*,' now it means only ' to swallow.'
In explaining how words gradually change their
meaning M. Arsène Darmesteter says, " L'histoire
des religions, des institutions sociales, politiques,
juridique, des idées morales, se ramène a ce
mouvement lent qui fait oublier aux habitudes
inconscientes de l'esprit le fait primordial, pour
ne plus voir que le fait secondaire qui en est
dérivé, et pour le changer en un fait primordial .
. . mais cette évolution est la loi génerale du
développement organique dans les êtres vivantes,
puisque le changement dans la vie se réduit le
plus habituellement à la disparition graduelle
de la cellule fondamentale devant la cellule
voisine qu'elle s'est peu à peu adjointe et qui
se développe à ses dépens."[1]

Applying this to our own problem we may
surmise that history took the following course.
First a word was used to signify those who,
having become a burden, were turned out of the
settlement.   Then it continued to be applied to
those who were put into a sheltered place to die.
Finally it was used to designate the dead body
that was carried to the same place for disposal.
It would seem that the word in its original sense,
meant someone who was useless, someone to be

[1] *La Vie des Mots* (11th Edition), p. 86.

got rid of; and as the grave was the direct descendant of the refuge, at last it was applied only to the dead. We are not without indications that this was so. Professor Fraser mentions a certain people.[1] among whom the very old are spoken of as dead, the same word being used for both. Again, a Somali, describing how he had been injured in a battle, said he had lain dead upon the field for some days. On being pressed by the Englishman to whom he was speaking he persisted in the use of the word ' dead.'

We arrive then at this conclusion. All the ancient facts connected with the ancient custom, the journey, the suffering from cold, the need of food and drink and weapons, the happy arrival at the older settlement, or the wretched existence of the outlaw—all these incidents in the life of the man who was cast out by the community cluster about the language of burial. Facts altered, but the words, of their legitimate descendants, remained and carried with them a burden of ancient history.

This, a mere sketch in outline with lights and shadows omitted, appears to furnish the missing link in my argument, and *mutatis mutandis* it applies to all methods of disposing of the dead except cremation.

[1] I have mislaid the reference.

CHAPTER XI.

THE LIFE OF THE DEAD.

Hitherto we have examined the various customs and beliefs concerning the Dead [1] mainly from the point of view of the Living. There exists, however, startling as it may appear, a very considerable body of information regarding the lives of the Dead from which it is possible to form a rough though fairly accurate idea of their existence after they were cast out by the Living. But in order to interpret clearly the signs and sayings that have reached us from so remote a past, we must bear in mind that they refer to three distinct methods of disposing of the unfit. The earliest of these, typified by the grotto at Aurignac, which was described in the first chapter, belongs to the nomad stage when a man who was but slightly injured, and who might reasonably be expected to recover, was put into shelter. As might be expected, there are few indications of what happened to him there ; for he lived

---

[1] For convenience, those who were cast out by the community will be referred to as the Dead, and those who cast them out as the Living, capital letters being used.

alone without intercourse with his fellow men
until he recovered sufficiently to join his tribe.
All we know is that he was provided with weapons,
food, and water, that precautions were taken
to indicate the route he should follow when he
emerged, and we have, perhaps, though this may
belong to a later stage, some account of his
rejoining his tribe.   We next come to the period
of emigration as distinguished from migration,
when pastoral or agricultural communities, more
or less settled, outgrew their means of subsistence
and threw out colonies. The most prominent
record of this stage is the sentence of banishment
which compelled the weaker colonists, who were
a burden in the new settlement, to return to the
parent village. Finally, we come to the time
when, from one cause or another, this practice
was discontinued, perhaps because communication with the older home had been cut off.   It
is in this period that we find the system of
outlawry in full force, although it began in the
previous stage when it was often a preliminary.
to banishment.

   Although these three customs have been allotted
to three distinct stages of human life, it must
not be supposed that they are separated in
tradition.   Not only is it natural for verbal
records to merge into one another, but in practice

the three customs ran concurrently. The primitive shelter, where the sick man was put to recover or die, developed in two directions, and its evolution on both lines may be traced without a break up to the present day. On the one hand it became a grave, or, when shelters were grouped, a cemetery : on the other it retained its original purpose. The sick and injured continued to be put in such shelters, where they were comparatively safe, and yet being out of the way of their fellows, were less troublesome to them. Here they were fed, as we have already seen, until they recovered, or until it became clear that they would not recover. On this line the shelter developed into our modern hospital where we put our sick, out of the way of those who are too busy earning a livelihood to look after them properly until they recover and rejoin their friends, or die and are carried to the cemetery. Similarly the primitive custom of food and water being deposited near the shelter by the sick man's friends has grown into a great organisation of doctors, nurses, chemists, and undertakers. So, in dealing with the records of the past we must not expect to find the three methods of disposal clearly separated.

A picturesque custom quoted by Tylor presents a realistic picture of the sentence of perpetual

excommunication.[1] " The Bodo of north-east
India thus celebrate the last funeral rites. The
friends repair to the grave, and the nearest
of kin to the deceased, taking an individual's
portion of food and drink, solemnly presents
it to the dead with the words, ' Take and eat,
heretofore you have eaten and drunk with us,
you can do so no more ; you were one of us,
you can be so no longer ; we come no more to
you, come you not to us.' Thereupon each of
the party breaks off a bracelet of thread
put on his wrist for the purpose, and casts
it into the grave." Though the meaning of
the ritual is obscure the words are unmistak-
able.

The sentence of exile or outlawry was often
strongly resented by the victim and had to be
enforced by the most rigorous methods. Customs
that record this are sometimes reduced to the last
stage of attenuation as among the Chuwashes in
Russia who fling a red-hot stone, after the corpse
is carried out, to bar the soul from returning.[2]
But the ceremonies may be far more elaborate.
For example, in Melanesia ghost hunts are
practised by various tribes, and neighbouring
villages are warned beforehand so that they may

[1] Tylor, *Primitive Culture*, vol. ii., p. 31.
[2] Tylor, *Primitive Culture*, vol. ii., p. 26.

take precautions to prevent the ghost taking
shelter among them.[1]

The difficult journey in the older home and the
doubtful reception they might meet on arrival
offered no agreeable prospect ; but even worse
was the outlook when there was no home to go
to, and the wretched man was driven forth into
the wild to join those who had been cast out before
him.   The wide-spread belief that the dead arrive
in the other world in the same state of body as
they left this, injured, or maimed, or weak,
shows that the exiled community were in no
position to give aid to new comers.   Indeed,
so dreadful was the prospect that many preferred
death to outlawry.   "The Fijians believe that
they enter the future life in the same state of
body as they leave this.   Therefore they used to
be anxious for death to come before old age or
disease disabled them.   So when a man felt the
approach of age he would ask his relations to
kill him, and it was considered a mark of affection
to strangle parents or other frail or sickly relatives,
or to knock them on the head with a club.   As
a rule it was left to the choice of the aged and
infirm to say whether they would prefer to be
buried alive or to be killed first and buried after-

[1] Sir J. G. Frazer, *Belief in Immortality*, vol. i., lecture
xvi., p. 357 (Macmillan, 1913).

wards. But the proposal to be put to death did not always emanate from the parties principally concerned : when a son, for example, thought that his parents were growing too old and becoming a burden to him, he would tell them it was time to die, a notice which was usually accepted with equanimity."[1]

A similar custom still prevails among the Chooktchi of Siberia, " The old people are put to death by their children, and so far as I could make out, the old people themselves take the initiative, for they believe this rite to be most acceptable to the gods, who will therefore give glory to the hunters and warriors. This ceremony took place twenty-five years ago not far from Nijne Kolymsk, and mention was made of it in the Yakutsk diocesan journal."[2] Traditions still exist among the Bouriats of the same practice, though it has long since been discontinued. Mr. Shklovsky after mentioning their migration into the Yakut country, continues, " This was probably in the thirteenth century. At that time the Bouriats had the custom of putting to death all the old people over seventy years of age : this ceremony was known as ' swallowing the fat '

[1] Sir J. G. Frazer, *Belief in Immortality*, vol. i., lecture xix., p. 422.
[2] Shklovsky, *In Far N.-E. Siberia*, p. 145, (Macmillan, 1916).

and is thus described. At the age of seventy the old man or woman gave a feast to the family and relations, and at the end of the feast the old person was forced to swallow a long ribbon of fat. Part of this was successfully swallowed, but the rest, remaining in the mouth, choked the victim.[1]

Mention has already been made of the custom of dividing funeral rites into two parts, the first of which takes place immediately after death, while the second is postponed until the lapse of several months or more. The former represents the act of outlawry only,[2] but the latter records two distinct customs. Sometimes as shown in Chapter V., it illustrates the sentence of banishment, when the outlaw was sent back to the older settlement, at a convenient season of the year. But when for one reason or another, the practice of banishment ceased, something had to be done with the outlaw. From many instances already quoted it is clear that for some time after sentence was passed it was customary to provide the outcast with food and other necessaries. He might recover and again become a useful member of his tribe. But it was impossible to support him indefinitely ; if he could be got rid of in no other

[1] *Ibid.*
[2] The period of outlawry appears to be recorded by the state of Purgatory.

way it appears that he was killed, and this may also have been the fate of those who refused to make the journey to the older settlement. " Among the Arunta of Central Australia the final mourning ceremony takes place some twelve to eighteen months after the death. It consists mainly in nothing more or less than a ghost hunt : men armed with shields and spear-throwers assemble and with loud shouts beat the air with the palms of their hands to chase away the dead man from the old camp which he loves to haunt. In this way the beaters gradually advance towards the grave till they have penned the ghost into it, when they immediately dance on the top of it, beating the air downwards as if to drive the spirit down, and stamping on the ground as if to trample him into the earth. After that the women gather round the grave and cut each other's heads with clubs till the blood streams down on it. This brings the period of mourning to an end. [1]

It is strange how customs linger on, even among civilised people, long after their intention is quite forgotten. In Europe the coffin is always carried out feet foremost, and, at least in England, it appears to be done without any definite

[1] Sir J. G. Frazer, *Belief in Immortality*, vol. i., lecture vii., p. 164 (Macmillan, 1913).

intention of meaning but merely because it is
customary. Elsewhere, as in Mabuiag, one of
the western islands of the Torres Straits, it is
believed that, if the corpse is not carried away
feet foremost, the ghost may return and trouble
the survivors.[1] Very probably the same belief
once lay at the root of the English custom.
But even so, the belief is as much a mystery as
the custom. Why should the mere fact of being
carried feet foremost prevent the ghost returning? Or, to translate the current belief into
its original terms, why should the mere fact
of carrying away the outlaw feet foremost prevent
his return to the community? I would suggest
that the act was intended as a warning and not
as a means of prevention : that the action was
symbolical, pertaining to the language of signs,
and that it was meant to indicate to the outlaw,
and to everybody else, that the community had
done with him once and for all. I suggest, for
verification by further research and comparison,
that the custom arose in this manner. In the
present day when a dead horse or other large
animal has to be dragged from one spot to another,
the most convenient way is to tie its legs together
and drag it with a rope—thus, necessarily, feet
foremost. Similiarly I suggest that the body of

[1] *Op. cit.*, vol. i., lecture viii., p. 174.

a dead man who was really dead, was dragged to
some distant place to decompose, or to be
devoured by birds and animals. So it may
have been that the outlaw with whom the
community intended to have no more dealings,
and perhaps after a violent struggle in which he
had been overcome, was bound and dragged
feet foremost out of the village. Where no
resistance was offered, as with the sick or sorely
injured, against whom there was no feeling
of animosity, but who yet had to be removed,
there was no reason to bind and drag them away,
and they might well be carried if unable to walk ;
but they must be carried feet foremost to indicate
that, like the dead, they must never come back
again.

Among the customs of ancient Gaul there
was one that casts a ray of light backwards
into what was even then a remote and forgotten
past. When the time came for the outcast to
be sent back to the older settlement it appears
that the opportunity was taken to communicate
through him with the friends and relations that
had stayed behind. Diodorus, Cæsar's contemporary, says, " At the burial of the dead, some
cast letters addressed to their departed relatives
upon the funeral pile, under the belief that
the dead will read them." Mela confirms this,

H

saying, " business accounts and payments of debt were passed on to the next world," while Valerius Maximus tells us that " money loans are given, to be repaid in the next world."[1] Here we have striking evidence of occasional intercourse between the emigrants and their friends at home, the outcast being employed as their messenger. But it deals with a period so remote that the Gauls of Cæsar's time had forgotten the true facts, and having in the interval adopted the custom of cremation, and also having acquired the art of writing, they burned the bills and letters on the funeral pile. So sure were the people of that earlier period that each when his turn came would be sent back to the older settlement, where he would meet those who had gone before, that, as we have just seen, loans were made to each other by the emigrants only to be repaid when they got back to the old home.

A similar custom exists in the present day among the Chooktchi. Mr. Shklovsky in describing the funeral of an old woman says, " The man leaped from the sledge and gave a packet to the son of the dead woman, saying something which I did not hear. Afterwards, I found that the man had owed some tobacco to a friend who subsequently died before the loan

[1] *Celtic Magazine*, 1886-7, p. 139.

was repaid, and the borrower now availed himself of this opportunity to return the tobacco by the old woman."[1]

In this instance also the woman was to be cremated. But the Chooktchi do not always burn their dead, for the same author tells us, " Sometimes the dead bodies, fully dressed, and with spears in their hands, are placed, together with all their ornaments and utensils, upon the snow-covered tundra, where the bodies are soon devoured by wolves and white polar foxes."[2]

There is evidence of an understanding between the Living and the Dead that some provision must be made by the former for the support of each new outcast. This will account, better than any theory of kindliness or humanity, which are modern virtues not too highly developed even in the present day, for the persistence of the custom of providing food and shelter, clothes and fire and weapons. The fee paid to Charon, and the practice not yet obsolete, of putting money in a dead man's mouth, or half-crowns on his eyes, are reminiscent of the fee paid to the outlaw community who demanded scot of all new-comers. " The people of Tumlco or Tamara, an island of Berlin Harbour in German New

[1] *In Far N.-E. Siberia*, p. 145, (Macmillan, 1916).
[2] Shklovsky, *In Far N.-E. Siberia*, p. 145.

Guinea believe that the *mos* or soul after death
goes to a place deep underground where there
is a great water. Over that water every soul
must pass on a ladder to reach the abode of bliss.
The ladder is in the keeping of a spirit called *Su
asin tjakin* or " the Great Evil," who takes toll
of the ghosts before he lets them use the ladder.
Hence an ear-ring and a bracelet are deposited
with every corpse in order that the dead man may
have wherewithal to pay the toll to the spirit
at the great water. Should the ghost try to cross
the ladder without paying toll the ghostly toll-
keeper tips the ladder up and the ghost falls
into the deep water and is drowned."[1]

It appears that the outlaws maintained the
tribal organisation to which they were accustomed,
and resented the intrusion of a member of another
tribe. " In the island of Florida, in Central
Melanesia, the ghosts are supposed to depart
by ship to the spirit-land. There they are met
by a ghost who thrusts a rod into their noses to
see whether the cartilage is pierced. Ghosts
whose noses have been duly bored in life follow
the onward path with ease, but all others have
pain and difficulty in making their way to the
realm of shades. . . . . Similarly at Bugotu in

[1] Sir J. G. Frazer, *Belief in Immortality*, vol. i., lecture x.,
p. 224 (Macmillan, 1913).

the Island of Ysabel (one of the Solomon Islands)
the ghosts of the dead are supposed to go away
to an island. In the island there is a pool with a
narrow tree-trunk lying across it. Here is
stationed Bolafagina, the ghostly lord of the
place. Every newly arrived ghost must appear
before him, and he examines their hands to see
whether they bear the mark of the sacred frigate-
bird cut in them : if so the ghosts pass across the
tree-trunk and mingle with the departed spirits
in the world of the dead. But ghosts who have
not the mark on their hands are cast into the gulf
and perish out of their ghostly life."[1] " The
Motu of Port Moresby in British New Guinea
cannot enter the realms of bliss unless their noses
have been pierced in their life-time. The operation is performed on children about the age of
six years ; and if children die before it has been
performed, the parents will bore a hole in the
nose of the corpse in order that the spirit of the
child may go to the happy land."[2]

A very pitiable fate was that of weak and sickly
children equally unwelcome among the Living
and the Dead. Kelly[3] quotes two folk-tales,

[1] Sir J. G. Frazer, *Belief in Immortality*, vol. i., lecture
xvi., p. 350 (Macmillan, 1913).
[2] *Ibid.*, vol. i., lecture ix., p. 193.
[3] Walter K. Kelly, *Curiosities of Indo-European Tradition
and Folk-Lore*, p. 131. (Chapman and Hall, 1863), quoting
Mannhardt, Die Gotterwelt der Deutschen und Nordischen
Volker, p. 291, Berlin 1860, and Robert Chambers, *Popular
Rhymes of Scotland*, p. 115, Edinburgh, 1847.

one German and one Scotch, which show that
those who were too young to help themselves
were rejected by the outcasts. "A Tyrolese
peasant, who was returning home at a late hour
on one of the 'twelve nights,' saw Perchta pass
by with her unchristened babes. All the little
ones had short white smocks, but that of the last
one was too long, and the child was continually treading upon it and tripping. 'Come
here, Draggle-tail,' said the peasant, 'and I'll
tie up your little skirt.' The child came to him,
and the man having taken off his garter and done
as he had promised, 'Oh, thank you,' said the
wee thing; 'now I have got a name,' and it
vanished, no doubt believing itself as good as
baptised.' That is the German story. The
scene of the Scotch story is laid at Whittinghame
in Scotland. "An unnatural mother having
murdered her child at a large tree not far from
the village, the ghost of the deceased was afterwards seen, on dark nights, running in a distracted
manner between the said tree and the churchyard, and was occasionally heard crying. The
villagers believed that it was obliged thus to take
the air, and bewail itself, on account of wanting
a name—no anonymous person, it seems, being
able to get a proper footing in the other world.
Nobody durst speak to the unhappy little spirit,

from a superstitious dread of dying immediately
after ; and to all appearance the village of
Whittinghame was destined to be haunted till
the end of time for want of an exorcist. At
length it fortunately happened that a drunkard,
one night on reeling home, encountered the
spirit, and being fearless in the strength of John
Barleycorn, did not hesitate to ·address it in the
same familiar style as if it had been one of his
own flesh-and-blood fellow topers. ' How's a'
wi' ye this morning, Short-Hoggers ? ' cried the
courageous villager ; when the ghost immediately
ran away, joyfully exclaiming :—

> Oh, weel's me noo, I've gotten a name ;
> They ca' me Short-Hoggers of Whittinghame.

And since that time it has never been either seen
or heard of. The name that the drunkard applied
to it denotes that the ghost wore short stockings
without feet."

A similar belief exists in the Isle of Man with
stillborn children. "There is a quaintly
charming story of an old Manxman passing
Arbory Church at midnight one Christmas Eve,
and as he came level with a great fuchsia hedge
which borders the vicarage garden, he heard
a soft low wailing, piteously insistent, coming
from the shadowy graveyard. As he drew nearer
and nearer, the trailing gentle murmur took

voice and words, the sad grieving lament of an unchristened · infant : 'Lhiannoo dyn ennym me ! ' (A child without name ám I !). The old man paused by the wall, and looking up towards the old kirk, he said clearly : ' My she gilley eu, ta mee bashtey eu Juan, as my she inneen eu ta me bashtey eu Joney.' (If thou art a boy I christen thee John, and if thou art a girl I christen thee Joney.) With a happy sigh, like the wind sinking to rest, the little ghost lay content and at peace." [1]

Without doubt we may interpret " un-christened " to mean " unnamed." The ceremony of naming, even in the present day among barbaric tribes, is not performed until a youth is old enough to hunt and fight and be a useful member of the community. The non-conformist adoption of adult baptism was merely a reversion to the older custom, which by a pro-cess resembling osmosis forced its way through the racial prejudice which separated the conquered people from their conquerors.

The meaning of the tales is now evident. Sick and weakly youths and children who were unlikely to recover were driven out by the community, as in later times the Spartans exposed those who were deformed. But evidently they

[1] Agnes Herbert, *The Isle of Man*, p. 185 (John Lane, 1909).

were equally unwelcome among the outcasts
where they would be a burden even greater.
So, admitted neither among the Living nor the
Dead, they wandered helplessly " between the
tree and the churchyard," that is, between the
settlement and the outlaws' refuges ; and no one
might have dealings with them because of the
taboo against the dead. In the draggle-tail
story the long smock of the child merely indicates
helplessness : it is nothing but corroborative detail
introduced in later times to emphasise the idea
of youth. The custom, not yet extinct, of
refusing to unbaptised children the right of burial
in consecrated ground, is apparently a reminiscence of those times.

Besides the existence of a tribal division among
the outcasts, already mentioned in this chapter,
there are indications of a primitive organisation.
In Ireland it is said to be the duty of the last man
buried to carry wood and water for the rest in
the other world [1] ; while among other people
he is supposed to become king until the next man
dies. But perhaps the implication merely is
that the last to be cast out of the settlement was
usually stronger than those who had suffered
outlawry for a longer time.

---

[1] Lady Wilde, *Ancient Legends of Ireland*, p. 82, 213.
See also Le Braz, *Legende de la Mort*, *passim*.

Perhaps the clearest indication that the so-called dead were living is the universal belief that they die. I have already quoted the belief of the people of Bugotu that those who have not the mark of the sacred frigate-bird on their hands are cast into the gulf and perish. Similarly among the natives of Saa in Malanta, another of the Solomon Islands, the dead are supposed to swim to an island; "but the life of the ghost is not eternal. The spirits of common people soon turn into the nests of white ants, which serve as food for the more robust ghosts. The ghosts of persons who were powerful on earth last much longer. So long as they are remembered and worshipped by the living their natural strength remains unabated; but when men forget them and no more food is offered to them in sacrifice, they pine away and change into white ants' nests just like common folk."[1] Again, the Koita of British New Guinea believe that the ghosts of the dead live a life very like the one they led on earth. But they do not live for ever; "for they grow weaker and weaker, and at last die the second death, never to revive again even as ghosts. There seems to be a notion that they survive only so long as their names and their

[1] Sir J. G. Frazer, *Belief in Immortality*, vol. i., lecture xvi., p. 350 (acmillan, 1913).

memories survive among the living. When they are utterly forgotten, the poor ghosts cease to exist. If that is so, it is obvious that the dead depend for their continued existence upon the recollection of the living." [1]

The Tami of German New Guinea believe that the soul of the deceased only departs to the lower world when the maggots swarm from his decaying body. [2] Some of the Indians of Guiana bring food and drink to their dead so long as the flesh remains on the bones ; but when it has mouldered away they conclude that the man himself has departed. The Matacos Indians of the Gran Chaco in Argentina believe that the soul of a dead man does not pass down into the nether world until his body is decomposed or burnt. Further, the Alfoors of Central Celebes suppose that the spirits of the departed cannot enter the spirit-land until all the flesh has been removed from their bones. . . . Messrs. Spencer and Gillen found that the tribes to the north of the Arunta (in Central Australia) regularly give their dead a second burial, that a change in the state of the ghosts is believed to coincide with the second burial, and apparently also, though this is not so definitely stated, that the time

---

[1] Sir J. G. Frazer, *The Belief in Immortality*, vol. i., p. 195.
[2] *Ibid.*, p. 166 (note).

for the second burial is determined by the disappearance of the flesh from the bones. Amongst the tribes which practise a second burial the custom is first to deposit the dead on platforms among the branches of trees till the flesh has quite mouldered away, and then to bury the bones in the earth. For example, in the Unmatjera and Kaitish tribes, when a man dies, his body is carried by his relations to a tree distant a mile or two from the camp. There it is laid on a platform by itself for some months. When the flesh has disappeared from the bones, a kinsman of the deceased, in strictness a younger brother, climbs up into the tree, dislocates the bones, places them in a wooden vessel, and hands them down to a female relative. Then the bones are laid in the grave with the head facing in the direction in which his mother's brother is supposed to have camped in the days of old. After the bones have been thus interred, the spirit of the dead man is believed to go away and to remain in the old *alcheringa* home.[1]

Among the Fijians it was believed possible to kill a troublesome ghost.[2] According to the Tami of New Guinea the souls of the dead live in the nether world. This spiritland is called Lamboam

---

[1] Sir J. G. Frazer, *The Belief in Immortality*, vol. i., p. 166.
[2] Sir J. G. Frazer, *Belief in Immortality*, vol. i., p. 415 (Macmillan, 1913).

and the entrance to it is by a cleft in a rock. Here everything is fairer and more beautiful than on earth ; fruits are plentiful, and the villages are full of ornamental plants. Life is very like that on earth : people work, and marry, and quarrel : they even fall sick and die. Souls that die are changed into vermin, such as ants and worms.[1]

We see in these later examples that the memory of shelter, outlawry, and exile has become confused. But with the knowledge already gained from other sources we can connect each with the conditions in which it originated. Also we can interpret the strange belief that the continued existence of the ghost of the dead is dependent on the memory of the living. When the community ceased to provide food for the outcasts they starved. And apparently the community soon forgot to do this unless means were taken to remind them ; for we saw that among the natives of Saa the ghosts of common people soon were devoured by white ants while those of persons who were powerful on earth, that is, those who were strong enough to make themselves feared lasted much longer. This receives further illustration among the Arunta. The last quotation from *The Belief in Immortality*

[1] *Ibid.*, p. 299.

given above ends thus : " But in these tribes very old men and women receive only one burial, being at once laid in an earthy grave and never set up on a platform in a tree ; and we have seen reason to think that this difference in the treatment of the aged springs from the indifference or contempt in which their ghosts are held by comparison with the ghosts of the young and vigorous."

CHAPTER XII.

Among the Fijians a main part of the ceremony
of a great man's funeral was the strangling of wives,
friends, and slaves, for the distinct purpose of
attending him into the world of spirits The
Caribs slay on the dead master's grave any of his
slaves they can lay hands on. Similar customs
are found in Central America, Mexico, and Bogota.

In Peru friends and dependents were invited
to immolate themselves and accompany the dead
man to the spirit world. In later times a llama
was substituted, the name of the supposed victim
being given to it.[1]

Of such funeral rites graphic and horrid descriptions are recorded in the countries across Africa—
East, Central, and West. A headman of the
Wadoe is buried sitting in a shallow pit, and with
the corpse a male and female slave alive, he with
a bill-hook in his hand to cut fuel for his lord
in the death-world, she seated on a little stool

---

[1] *The Incas of Peru.* Sir Clements Markham, chap. viii.,
p. 111 (Smith Elder, 1910).

with the dead chief's head in her lap. A chief of Unyamwezi is entombed in a vaulted pit, sitting on a low stool with a bow in his right hand, and provided with a pot of native beer ; with him are shut in alive three women. [1]

The King of Dahome must enter Deadland with a ghostly court of hundreds of wives, eunuchs, singers, drummers, and soldiers. In southern districts of Africa, accounts of the same class begin in Congo and Angola with the recorded slaying of the dead man's favourite wives to live with him in the other world a practice still in vogue among the Chevas of the Zambesi district, and formerly known among the Maravis ; while the funeral sacrifice of attendants with a chief is a thing of the past among the Barotse ; as among the Zulus, who yet have not forgotten the days when the chief's servants and attendant warriors were cast into the fire which had consumed his body, that they might go with him, and prepare things before-hand, and get food for him. Marco Polo records that when the King of Maabar dies his body is burnt and his guard of horsemen throw themselves into the fire to do him service in the next world. In the Seventeenth Century the practice is described as still prevailing in Japan, where, on the death

[1] Tylor, *Primitive Culture*, vol. i., p. 459, *et seq.*

of a nobleman, from ten to thirty of his servants put themselves to death by ' hara kari.' Any-one met on the road by the funeral of a Mongol prince was slain and ordered to go as escort. In the Kimbunda country any one who meets a royal funeral procession is put to death with the other victims at the grave.[1] The Shinto method of disposing of the dead is by burial, cremation having been introduced into Japan with Buddhism. Wives and others were sacrificed at the grave, and food and ornaments were buried with the dead. Shoes also have been found in the graves

Tylor comments on these customs in a way which disposes of the matter without making it any clearer. He says : " When a man of rank dies and his soul departs to its own place it is a rational inference of early philosophy that the soul of attendants, slaves, and wives, put to death at his funeral, will make the same journey and continue their service in the next life." Unfortunately we know nothing of early philosophy, and we have no reason to assume that it corresponded with the philosophy of primitive people in the present day. His mistake arises from the common error that people adopt customs because they hold certain beliefs. The

[1] Tylor *Primitive Culture*, vol. i., pp. 4, 61 *et seq.*

I

reverse of this is the truth, beliefs being the traditional explanations of customs.

It is undoubtedly a fact that customs develop. A Lord Mayor's show is a much more elaborate affair than it was in the days when London could shut its gates in the face of kings. They grow even after their original intention has been forgotten : indeed they grow more luxuriously for they are then free to assimilate things that are really foreign to them. While they have a meaning which everyone understands, and a use which is obviously practical, there is a check upon their growth : but once they become a mere ceremony—a Lord Mayor's show—there is none.

On these grounds we might argue, with some appearance of reason, that the sacrifice of slaves and attendants was no more than an amplification in later times, when the meaning was forgotten, of the earlier custom of providing the injured man with things that were necessary for his journey. There is however an insuperable objection to this argument. The slaves are killed—deliberately slaughtered—and that, without further explanation, forms a break in the history of the custom. Once the custom of killing slaves for the use of the dead man was established one can easily understand that, as the community grew more prosperous, more and more were sacrificed. The difficulty is to account for the beginning. Up to a certain period only clothes, food, and weapons were offered, then suddenly, without apparent reason, people decided to kill a slave. Why?

There is, of course, the well known custom of breaking or destroying offerings before they are thrown into the grave ; and it might be claimed that the killing of slaves followed by analogy. But the destruction of the funeral offerings offers almost precisely the same difficulty as the slaughter of slaves ; so we should only be explaining one difficulty by something that is not understood.

Tylor says : "It will appear from the ethnography of this rite, (the slaughter of attendants), that it is not strongly marked in the very lowest levels of culture, but that, arising in the lower barbaric stage, it develops itself in the higher."[1] MacCulloch, summarises the results of investigation in the Celtic area thus. " Over the whole Celtic area a rich profusion of grave-goods has been found, consisting of weapons, armour, chariots, utensils, ornaments, and coins. Some of the interments undoubtedly point to sacrifice of wife, children, or slaves at the grave. Male and female skeletons are often in close

[1] Tylor, *Primitive Culture*, vol. i., p. 458..

proximity, in one case the arm of the male encircling the neck of the female. In other cases the remains of children are found with these. Or while the lower interment is richly provided with grave goods, above it lie irregularly several skeletons, without grave goods, and often with the head separated from the body, pointing to decapitation, while in one case the arms had been tied behind the back."[1]   The latter quotation is a miscellaneous collection of facts rather than a summary ; but, taken with the extract from Tylor we get the general impression of a gradual and continuous change of custom. In the earlier chapter on funeral offerings I showed how the more simple offerings may be accounted for by the needs of the wounded hunter in the grotto at Aurignac. That was in the very early period of constant migration. Subsequent chapters showed how emigration, exodus, and progress in material culture all had their influence on the disposal of those whose presence handicapped their fellows : how, as settlements succeeded temporary camps, the useless were driven out instead of being left behind : how exodus before an intrusive race made a return to the older home impossible, with the result that the outlaws lived on the outer fringe of the

[1] MacCulloch, *Religion of the Ancient Celts*, p. 337.

community, necessitating stern measures to prevent their return. As an extension of the custom of giving the outlaw the means of earning his subsistence, the inclusion of wives, attendants, and slaves offers no difficulty : with the growth of the conception of personal property it would be a natural, almost a necessary extension—provided they were taken away alive. But we can also understand that there may have been some reluctance on the part of a man's dependents to follow him into outlawry. If they were allowed to remain in the settlement it would be an infringement of the rights of the outlaws, while there would also be the possibility of their conniving at the return of their outlawed master. The only thing was to drive them out, with violence if necessary, and to kill them if they returned. Tylor mentions a funeral ceremony that appears to bear this out. " Among the rude Kayans of Borneo, slaves are killed in order that they may follow the deceased and attend upon him. Before they are killed the relations who surround them enjoin them to take care of their master when they join him. . . . The female relatives of the deceased then take a spear and slightly wound the victims, after which the males spear them to death."[1]

[1] Tylor, *Primitive Culture*, vol. i., p. 458.

A custom, somewhat similar, in which the victims are not actually killed but are left to die in the company of the deceased, is more evidently a survival of the age when attendants accompanied their master. " Here are details from an account published in 1849 of the funeral of a late King of Cochin China. When the corpse of Thien Tri was deposited in the coffin, there were also deposited in it many things for the use of the deceased in the other world, such as crowns, turbans, clothes of all descriptions, gold, silver, and other precious articles, rice and other provisions . . . meals were set out near the coffin. In the tomb, an enclosed edifice of stone, the childless wives of the deceased were to be perpetually shut up to guard the sepulchre, and prepare daily the food and other things of which they think the deceased has need in the other life."[1]

I have mentioned incidentally the custom of breaking the offerings before putting them in the grave. In the light of previous chapters this does not appear to need much explanation ; for it is unlikely, at least in the earliest times, that the people gave of their best to those they were driving out of the community.

But the custom of destroying the property of the deceased had yet another origin. Perpetual

[1] Tylor *Primitive Culture*, vol. i., p. 489.

disagreements appear to have existed between the Living and the Dead, and a fruitful cause was disputes about property, whether personal or communal. However little personal rights a man may have had in property, at least the food that he was in the act of eating was regarded as his own. In Mabuiag, one of the western islands of the Torres Straits, when the body has been laid upon a stage or platform on clear, level ground away from the dwelling, the remains of any food and water of which the deceased might have been partaking in his last moments was carried out and placed beside the corpse lest the ghost should come back to fetch them for himself, to the annoyance and terror of his relations.[1] Again, a woman was not separated from her infant child. In Melanesia if the woman dies and the child lives, her ghost will not go away to the nether world without taking the infant with her. Hence in order to deceive the ghost, they wrap a piece of banana trunk loosely in leaves and lay it on the bosom of the dead mother when they lower her into the grave. She is not supposed to discover her loss at once, and before she has time to come back for it the child is removed to another house.[2] Communal,

---

[1] Sir J. G. Frazer, *Belief in Immortality*, vol. i., p. 174.
[2] Sir J. G. Frazer, *Belief in Immortality*, vol. i., p. 358.

or at least family, ownership appears to be indicated by the custom mentioned earlier in this volume of dividing a dead man's property so that he, as well as the survivors, each get an equal share : the outcast was entitled to take away with him his own portion of the public wealth. Similarly the examples quoted in the previous chapter seem to show that the other outcasts claimed certain rights in what he brought with him. The fact of their refusing him admission to the society unless he paid a fee shows that the right to private ownership was not absolute. The idea was one of slow growth and has never been fully accepted ; for taxation, and the entrance fees and subscriptions to clubs and societies are based on the principle that certain rights in a man's property still remain vested in the public. Frazer quotes a belief of the people of the Gazelle Peninsular in New Britain, " On arriving at the islands which are the home of departed spirits a dead man is asked how much shell money he left behind him. If it was little or none he is sent back and prowls about the village at night where he seeks to avenge himself by scaring or plaguing survivors. His relations or friends sometimes set food for him to devour, and if somebody takes pity on him, gives a feast in his honour and distributes shell money to the guests, the ghost may return to the island of the dead.[1]

But even if his food and clothes, weapons and other portable possessions were surrendered to the outcast there still remained property that could not be carried away by him and whether the ownership on this was communal and the outcast could only claim his share, or whether his rights in it were personal, this real estate remained a source of contention. Apparently the only means that early man could devise to put an end to quarrels on this score was to destroy the property. In Mabuiag, one of the western islands of the Torres Straits, on the day of death the mourners went into the gardens, slashed at the taro, knocked down coco-nuts, pulled up sweet potatoes, and destroyed bananas. We are told that " the food was destroyed for the sake of the dead man ; it was like good-bye." We may suspect, says Sir J. Frazer, that the real motive for the destruction was the same as that for laying food and water beside the corpse, namely, a wish to give the ghost no excuse for returning.[2]

[1] Sir J. G. Frazer, *Belief in Immortality*, vol. i., p. 406.
[2] *Belief in Immortality*, vol. i., p. 174.

CHAPTER XIII.

GHOSTS.

The universal belief in ghosts has never been satisfactorily explained. Tylor says, " That the apparitional soul bears the likeness of its fleshy body, is the principle implicitly accepted by all who believe it really and objectively present in dreams and visions. My own view is that nothing but dreams and visions could have ever put into men's minds such an idea as that of souls being ethereal images of bodies."[1] In modern belief, although the ghost has become more ethereal and intangible, it still retains some bodily characteristics: it speaks, though its voice is hollow; it is clothed, though sometimes only in a shroud; and often it drags chains or carries a dagger. According to the Irish sagas, " the dead who return are not spectres, but are fully clothed upon with a body. Thus when Cuchulainn returns at the command of St. Patrick, he is described exactly as if he were still in the flesh. ' His hair was thick and black . .

[1] Tylor, *Primitive Culture*, vol. i., p. 450.

in his head his eye gleamed swift and grey. . .
Blacker than the side of a cooking spit each of
his two brows, redder than ruby his lips.'"[1]
Le Braz sums up the Breton belief : " Ailleurs,
nous voyons le fantôme d'un laboureur pousser
la charrue, ou bien c'est le rouet d'un vieux
fileur d'étoupes qui se fait entendre, après sa mort
aussi obstiné que de son vivant. Ces êtres
d'outre-tombe sont désignés par un nom collectif :
ann Anaon, les Ames. Mais ces âmes n'apparais-
sent point séparées de leur corps. Le défunt
garde sa forme matérielle, son extérieur physique,
tous ses traits. Il garde aussi son vêtement
contumier ; il porte la même veste de travail,
le même feutre à larges bords qu'on lui a connus,
quand il était de ce monde. Et ses sentiments
non plus ni ses goûts, ni ses préoccupations, ni
ses intérêts ne sont devenus autres. Les idées
chrétiennes n'ont pu entamer sur ce point la
vieille croyance primitive. Le mort a ses sym-
pathies et ses aversions, ses amours et ses haines.
Un manque d'égards le met hors de lui ; si on lui
fait du tort, il se venge. Son âpreté paysanne ne
l'abandonne pas, ni davantage, il est vrai, le
souvenir des dettes qu'il a laissées impayées
et dont, au reste, il ne s'acquitte pas moins

---

[1] MacCulloch. *Religion of the Ancient Celts*, p. 336, and
The Celtic Magazine, 1886-7, p. 139.

religieusement que ne faisait le Celte du temps des druides. Comme de son vivant, il se passione, fermier, pour son champ, pêcheur, pour sa barque et pour ses filets. Sa maison, il la hante presque autant que par le passé. Il revient s'asseoir dans l'âtre, chauffer ses peids à la braise, converser avec les servantes, surveiller le train des gens et celui des choses."[1]

MacCulloch arrives very nearly at the truth when he says, " The world of the dead was in all respects a replica of this world. . . . In existing Breton and Irish belief the dead resume their tools, crafts, and occupations, and they preserve their old feelings. Hence, when they appear on earth, it is in bodily form and in their customary dress."[2]

In the light of previous chapters it is at once apparent that the belief in ghosts is a record of the constant efforts to return to the community of those who had been driven out. The wandering ghosts of Europe are usually those of murderers, or persons who have left worldly business un-finished—pledges unredeemed, debts unpaid, heirs defrauded, treasure concealed ; in short violent men reckless of the anger of the community, or those whose needs and anxieties drove them to

[1] *La Legende de la Mort*, Anatole Le Braz (1912), vol. i., p. xlvi.
[2] *Religion of the Ancient Celts*, p. 344.

risk a visit to their home. In northern Melanesia sometimes when a man dies and his soul arrives in the spirit land, his friends do not want him there and drive him back to earth, so he comes to life again. That is the explanation which the natives give of recovery after a faint or swoon.[1] The popular belief in the Gazelle Peninsular has been mentioned already that the dead man who arrives without shell money at the home of departed spirits is sent back to the survivors, and scares them till they provide him with enough to ensure his reception among the dead. Similarly the European belief in the return of the ghost in search of buried treasure implies that the man who was driven out of the community had a customary right to his own property, or at least to a share of it. The custom of repaying debts due to the dead, formerly practised by the Celts and still by the Chooktai of north eastern Siberia[2] no doubt originated as a precaution to prevent the outcast returning to claim his dues.

But the cardinal reason all over the world for the return of the ghost is the omission of funeral rites. This was evidently regarded both by the Living and the Dead as a justifiable reason for returning. To furnish shelter for the man who

[1] Sir J. G. Frazer, *Belief in Immortality*, vol. i., p. 405.
[2] Shklovsky, *In Far North-East Siberia*, p. 145 (Macmillan, 1916).

was driven out, and provision for his journey
to the older settlement, was a duty incumbent on
the community and enforced by public opinion.
Every man knew that his turn would come some
day, so all would be in favour of its strict
observance.

Another common form of ghost is that of a
murdered man or one who has died a violent
death, and it is frequently the custom to build
a cairn over their graves to prevent them from
' walking.'   At first sight it may appear impossible
to make these facts fit in with my theory of the
origin of graves ; yet it is, as I will show, an
illuminating illustration of its truth. Great
discoveries become the truisms of later generations ; one of these is that man is mortal. In
very early times men did not live to see old age,
dangers surrounded them too closely. Only the
strong could hope to escape them ; so even
disease was in all probability only the preliminary
to a death by violence. But, as we have seen,
the injured and the ill were such a burden to their
friends that their presence was intolerable and
they were excommunicated. When, in comparatively recent times, it became possible for men to
reach old age, their death from no apparent cause
must have seemed to be an inexplicable phenomenon. Yet it occurred—more and more frequently,

until at last it was evident that men could die of age. But there were no earlier traditions of this form of death. Those who had been driven out in ancient times were not dead in our meaning of the word. Tradition told of their journey, of their life 'outside,' and, under the name of ghosts, of their unwelcome return. None of these things were connected with those who died of old age, so we get the old Irish belief that only those who die of old age are really dead. Those who died of old age and were buried in the ancient refuges did not return ; but men who had been struck by a stone axe might recover, and doubtless often did recover. In modern warfare it is no uncommon thing for a soldier, left for dead upon the battlefield, to regain consciousness and crawl back to join his regiment. Yet modern weapons are far more deadly than the primitive stone axe that might stun without killing. The inefficiency of primitive weapons was so well known that we have the modern savage custom of cutting off the thumb of a slain foe ' so that its ghost may not be able to wield an axe.' One of the grievances that the Somalis have against the European is that of selling them fire-arms that kill. When wounded with a spear a man more frequently recovered and consequently there were fewer blood-feuds. So the Irish belief amounts to this : men recover from wounds but not from old age.

The custom of building cairns over the graves of those who die a violent death, that is to say, the only form of death known to primitive man, is now easy to understand. The cairn was the mound over the subterranean refuge ; in Egypt its whole history has been traced from a mere heap of stones covering and protecting the refuge, to the great pyramids of the Dynastic period. The cairn then is the last remnant in modern practice of the ancient refuge for the injured man where he was put to recover or to die, and in building a cairn over the grave of one who has died by violence we are merely continuing the old custom for the old form of death.

It has been shown that those who were driven out from the community were constantly endeavouring to return in spite of every effort to prevent them. Their most favourable opportunity for evading the vigilance of those within the pale was evidently during the hours of darkness, and that precisely is the time when ghosts are said to walk : at dawn they vanish : cock-crow is the signal for their retreat. " The Hurons believe that the dead man's soul comes and walks by night in the village, and eats the remnants in the kettles."[1] "The Karens of Burma believe that the spirits of the dead may come up from the land of shades by night, but at daybreak must return."[2] "The souls of the Samoan Islanders come up during the hours of darkness to revisit their former abodes, retiring at dawn to the bush or to the lower regions."[3]

"Invisible le jour, mais non absentes, les âmes, dès le coucher du soleil, envahissent les champs, les landes, les chemins, pour vaquer à leur silencieuses besognes. . . . Elles rôdent autour des maisons, elles y pénètrent, elles s'y installent jusqu'au premier chant du coq."[4] Among the Kai of German New Guinea the ghosts are believed to sleep by day and go about their business by night. It is easy to scare them away by means of fire. That is why no native will go even a short way in the dark without a bamboo torch.[5]

This practice of appearing only during the hours of darkness may have been the origin of the strange stories about men with no shadow. Primitive language was essentially concrete—

[1] Tylor, *Primitive Culture*, vol. ii., p. 30.
[2]   ditto   ditto   vol. ii., p. 67.
[3]   ditto   ditto   vol. ii., p. 50.
[4] *Legende de la Mort*, Le Braz, vol. i., p. xlix.
[5] Sir J. G. Frazer, *Belief in Immortality*, vol. 1, p. 282.

K

what Sir A. Quiller Couch calls masculine
language :—

> " Masculine will always be
>
> Things that you can touch and see."

Abstract terms came later. For example there
is the old French expression for ' twilight,'
entre chien et loup. I would suggest, though
very tentatively, that as ' between dog and wolf '
meant ' twilight,' so ' no shadow ' meant ' night.'
But if this interpretation is correct we see how
easily the meaning of such expressions are
forgotten, and with what absurd results. We
are told that the dead in Purgatory knew that
Dante was alive when they saw that, unlike
their's, his figure cast a shadow on the ground.
Yet it was because the dead (the outcasts) only
left their shelters by night that they threw no
shadow, and Dante when he entered their dark
abode would have none either.

The vampire, which is the ghost of a dead man,
goes out from its buried corpse and sucks the
blood of living men. The corpse may be
recognised because it remains fresh, supple, and
ruddy ; it will bleed when cut, and even move
or shriek. Here clearly is a memory of the time
when the ' buried ' were not corpses, but living
beings who in their need for food crept out at night
when men were sleeping and sucked the blood of

their victims. The traditional method of laying a vampire strengthens this assumption, for it should be staked down, or its head should be cut off ; that is to say it must be killed.

Superstitions regarding incubi and succubi now offer no difficulty. They merely indicate that the outcasts, as might be expected, retained their sexual desires.

As life became easier these visits appear to have been tolerated. " Longtemps ce fut un usage, en Bretagne, de ne point verroniller les portes, la nuit, en prevision de la venue possible des morts. Aujourd'hui encore, on a soin de couvrer de cendre la braise de l'âtre, pour qu'ils soient assurés de trouver du feu à toute heure. Et les aliments qu'on dispose ou qu'on laisse sur la table, le soir de certaines fêtes, répondent à la même préoccupation."

" Par une espèce d'accord tacite, il est entendu que la terre appartient, le jour, aux vivants, la nuit aux morts. Et le pacte veut être respecté de part et d'autre. Le vivant qui le rompt s'expose à de fâcheuses rencontres, susceptibles d'entrainer les plus funestes conséquences. Mais le mort, de son côte, ne peut l'enfreindre sans dommage : lequel ? On ne nous le dit pas de façon explicite. Mais nous voyons constamment les âmes errantes trembler d'être surprises par le jour. Une puissance supérieure—celle de Dieu, déclara le christianisme—les contraint de regagner, souvent à regret, les résidences diurnes qui leur sont assignées." [1]

But this toleration had its limits, and the community could at any time enforce the outlawry if the Dead took undue advantage of the facilities conceded to them.   An illustration of this is given by Hartland.[2] " The ancient Scandanavians seem to have instituted solemn legal proceedings against troublesome ghosts. There is a remarkable story in the Eyrbyggja Saga of a number of malignant ghosts who haunted the settlement of Frodiswater . . . who had audaciously come and sat by the fires . . . and devasted the place with sickness and misfortune.   The ghosts were summoned to a doordoom ; and it was done in all manners even as at a doom of the thing : verdicts were delivered, cases summed up, and doom given.   The ghosts attended in obedience to the summons.   As each was found guilty he was sentenced to depart. . . . Thus they were banished one after another." [3]

It is one thing to drive a man away, but quite another matter to keep him from returning.

[1] Le Braz, *Legende de la Mort*, vol. 1, p. xlix.
[2] Hartland, *Ritual and Belief*, p. 187.
   Tylor, *Primitive Culture*, vol. ii., p. 27.

Violence was used when necessary, but apparently with reluctance due, perhaps, less to kindness than to fear of reprisals. " The Blanchwater section of the Dieri tribe fear the spirits of the dead and accordingly take steps to prevent their resurrection. For that purpose they tie the toes of the corpse together and the thumbs behind the back."[1]

But force may be evaded by cunning and great ingenuity was displayed in making the return more difficult. There is the well known custom of carrying away the body by a circuitous route. Crossing water to break the trail was another method. After burying a body the Ngarigo were wont to cross a river to prevent the ghost from pursuing them[2]; and this custom, in its last stage before disappearance, is recorded in the Roman rite of carrying water in a dish round the mourners after a funeral. The Wakelbura marked all the trees in circle round the place where the dead man was buried, so that when he emerged from the grave and set off in pursuit of his retiring relations, he would follow the marks on the trees in a circle and always come back to the point from which he had started.[3]

---

[1] Sir J. G. Frazer, *Belief in Immortality*, vol. i., p. 144.
[2] *Ibid*, p. 152.
[3] Sir J. G. Frazer, *Belief in Immortality*, vol. 1, p. 152.

If in spite of all precautions the man succeeded in making his way back, it was possible to detect his presence in various ways. The Blanchwater people just mentioned, sweep a clear space round the grave at dusk every evening and if they find any tracks on it, they assume they have been made by the restless ghost in his nocturnal peregrinations.[1] The Philippine Islanders, and the Hos of North-East India, sprinkle ashes at the threshold of their dwellings for the same purpose,[2] while among the Brandenburg peasants it is usual to pour out a pail of water at the door after the coffin.[3]

Yet those precautions did not suffice. Measures were necessary against those within the tribe who, from good nature or for other reasons, were tempted to assist the outlaws. By the tribal law there must be no friendship between those within the pale and those without. There is the Breton story of a mother meeting the spirit of her dead son at his grave. She went towards him with open arms ; but he waived her off saying : " We must not kiss."[4] In a footnote Le Braz adds, " Dans les contes irlandais (Fireside stories of Ireland, p. 61-62) un homme qui

---

[1] Sir J. G. Frazer, *The Belief in Immortality*, vol. i., p. 144.
[2] Tylor, *Primitive Culture*, vol. ii. p. 197.
[3] *Ibid*, vol. ii., p. 27.
[4] Le Braz, *Legende de la Mort*, vol. ii., p. 100.

revient d'un château enchanté et rentre chez
ses parents ne doit ni donner ni recevoir de
baiser."

To eat together is a very ancient and wide-
spread sign of friendship, and many tales recall
the rule that those who eat the food of the ' dead '
may not return to the ' living '—those who ate
with the outlaws were outlawed in their turn.

Le Braz quotes an example from *Celtic Folk-
lore* by Rhys: " A l'île de man, un homme
franchit le seuil d'une salle où les fées
banquetaient ; parmi les convives, il reconnaît
des personnes de sa connaissance. L'une d'elles
l'avertit charitablement de ne goûter à rien de
ce qu'on pourra lui offrir, s'il ne veut s'exposer
à ne jamais revoir sa demeure. La personne
qui lui avait donné ce salutaire conseil était un
mort." One or two examples from Tylor's
Primitive Culture [1] will suffice to indicate how
wide spread is this food tabu which hitherto
has always proved a mystery. " One of the most
characteristic of these savage narratives is from
New Zealand. This story, which has an especial
interest from the reminiscence it contains of the
gigantic Moa, and which may be repeated at some
length as an illustration of the minute detail and
life-like reality which such visionary legends

[1] *Op cit*, vol. ii., p. 50.

assume in barbaric life, was told to Mr. Shortland
by a servant of his named Te Wharewera. An
aunt of this man died in a solitary hut near the
banks of Lake Rotorua. Being a lady of rank
she was left in her hut, the door and windows
were made fast, and the dwelling was abandoned,
as her death had made it tapu. But a day or
two after, Te Wharewera with some others
paddling in a canoe near the place at early
morning saw a figure on the shore beckoning to
them. It was the aunt come to life again, but
weak and cold and famished. When sufficiently
restored by their timely help, she told her story.
Leaving her body, her spirit had taken flight
toward the North Cape, and arrived at the
entrance of Reigna. There, holding on by the
stem of the creeping akeake-plant, she descended
the precipice, and found herself on the sandy
beach of a river. Looking round, she espied
in the distance an enormous bird, taller than a
man, coming towards her with rapid strides.
This terrible object so frightened her, that her
first thought was to try to return up the steep
cliff; but seeing an old man paddling a small
canoe towards her she ran to meet him, and so
escaped the bird. When she had been safely
ferried across she asked the old Charon,
mentioning the name of her family, where the

spirits of her kindred dwelt. Following the path the old man pointed out, she was surprised to find just such a path as she had been used to on earth ; the aspect of the country, the trees, shrubs, and plants were all familiar to her. She reached the village and among the crowd assembled there she found her father and many near relations ; they saluted her, and welcomed her with the wailing chant which Maoris always address to people met after long absence. But when her father had asked about his living relatives, and especially about her own child, he told her she must go back to earth, for no one was left to take care of his grandchild. By his orders she refused to touch the food that the dead people offered her." Tylor adds the following note. " The idea, of which the classic representative belongs to the myth of Persephone, that the living who tasted the food of the dead may not return, and which is so clearly stated in this Maori story, appears again among the Sioux of North America. Ahak-tah seems to die, but after two days comes down from the funeral-scaffold where his body has been laid, and tells his tale. His soul had travelled by the path of braves through the beautiful land of great trees and gay loud-singing birds, till he reached the river, and saw the homes of the spirits of his forefathers on the shore beyond. Swimming across, he entered the nearest house, where he found his uncle sitting in a corner. Very hungry, he noticed some wild rice in a bark dish. " I asked my uncle for some rice to eat, but he did not give it to me. Had I eaten of the food for spirits, I never should have returned to earth."

The attempt to evade the tribal law against communication between their members and the living are further illustrated by the Breton belief that only those who will die within the year are able to see the souls of the dead. Translated to its early meaning this would run : only those who are not far from death, that is, the sick and injured, those in short who soon will be outlawed themselves have dealings with the outlaws. What a comment on human nature ! The strong and healthy maintain the tribal sentence in all its rigour against the outlaws ; but those who know that they will soon be driven out themselves are ready to propitiate the men who shortly will be their companions. And as to the outlaws—they dare not face the strong men of the tribes, but take advantage of the feeble.

CHAPTER XIV.

ANCESTOR WORSHIP.

It has already been suggested that the decreasing severity displayed in the treatment of those who were driven out of the community must not be attributed entirely to good nature. Disinterested kindness on the part of an individual is only tolerated when it does not injure the community: when the public gains thereby it becomes a recognised virtue. It would seem, then, that the gradual change in attitude towards the outcasts, a change from hostility, through toleration, to one of open benevolence, implies that it was found desirable to cultivate their goodwill. It is not unlikely that those who lived on the outskirts of the community served as a kind of buffer state between them and neighbouring hostile tribes, or rather, as a chain of outposts who would give timely warning in case of attack. We appear to have records of this both in burial customs and in popular beliefs about mythical heroes. " It was a custom in Ireland to bury the dead warrior in his armour, fully armed, and facing the region whence enemies might be expected. Thus he was a perpetual menace to them and prevented their attack." [1] Then we have Celtic tales of heroes " who departed to mysterious islands or to the hollow hills where they lie asleep, but whence they will one day return to benefit their people. So Arthur passed to Avalon, but in other tales he and his warriors are asleep beneath Craig-y-Delinas, just as Fionn and his men rest within this or that hill in the Highlands. Similar legends are told of other Celtic heroes, and they witness to the belief that great men who had died would return in the hour of their people's need. In time they were thought not to have died at all, but to be merely sleeping and waiting for their hour. The belief is based on the idea that the dead are alive in grave or barrow, or in a spacious land below the earth." [2]

In New Guinea it would be thought very unlucky if all the ancestral ghosts deserted the settlement [3]; and Le Braz notes that the Bretons dislike putting grave yards far from the village. This may have been for reasons of protection, or perhaps merely for convenience ; for, in extracts already quoted from *La Legende de la Mort*, it has been shown that according to Breton

[1] MacCulloch, *Religion of the Ancient Celts*, p. 338.
[2] *Ibid.*, p. 344.
[3] *Handbook of Folk-Lore*, p. 84.

folk-lore the dead come sometimes and labour in the fields by night. Among the Roro-speaking tribes at the mouth of the St. Joseph river in British New Guinea although the ghosts of the dead are greatly feared, it is said that if they abandoned a village altogether the luck of the villagers would be gone, and if such a thing is supposed to have happened, measures are taken to bring back the spirits of the departed to the old home. [1]

Another example of their usefulness is recorded in a custom of the Veddas. " The true basis of Vedda religion is the cult of the ordinary dead man —of their own dead, now become *Yaku* or ghosts. The jungle is haunted by them. They are regarded as friends and fellows. The charms which accompany ritual feasts are prayers asking them to come and share the meal, for ' we also eat and drink ' the same food. In each little community there is one man, the *Kapurale*, who has the power and knowledge needed to call the *Yaku*. He invokes the chief of the *Yaku*, Kande Yaka, and requests him to bring the *Nae Yaka*, or lately deceased person, along with him. The *Nae Yaka* speaks through the *Kapurale*, promising help in hunting and the like." [2]

[1] Sir J. G. Frazer, *Belief in Immortality*, vol. i., p. 198.
[2] *Handbook of Folk-Lore*, p. 87.

But perhaps more than in any other way it was by advice in times of difficulty that their help was most valuable. Many, perhaps the majority, of those who were expelled were past the prime of life—the elders of the community, possessing the knowledge that comes by years, the wisdom gained by experience, and bearers of the ancient traditions. As Saul in his trouble went to the witch of Endor to ask counsel of the ghost of Samuel, so it is not irrational to suppose that primitive man called on the exiled elders for advice ; and there are records of this state of things. In the chapter on the life of the Dead a description was given of the ceremony called ' swallowing the fat ' by which the Bouriats of Siberia in earlier times disposed of their dead by choking them. The ·traditional reason for the discontinuance of this custom is that the advice of old people was found useful.[1] Mr. W. Crooke speaks of the existence in Brittany of a trade called ' listener to the dead.' " The Breton folk believe that the dead watch all the acts of their descendants. The peasants never take an important decision without asking the approval of their forbears. Thus there has grown up an occupation of interpreting to the living the wishes of the dead. One of these listeners

[1] Shklovsky, *In Far North-East Siberia*, p. 145.

to the dead died in a village near Lorient in 1913."[1]

A similar custom exists among the Tami who inhabit a group of islands off the mainland of New Guinea. They believe that the ghosts of the departed return to their homes in the shape of serpents which have lost the faculty of speech and can only express themselves in whistles. These whistles the seer, who is generally a woman, can understand. It is even possible for men, and especially for women, to go down alive into the nether world. Women who possess this faculty transmit it to their daughters so that the profession is hereditary. To effect this they rub their foreheads with ginger and lie down on the dead man's property and go to sleep.[2] Another tribe of New Guinea make white marks on their foreheads by which they believe they can enter into communication with the spirits of the departed.

These marks on the forehead would appear to be in the relic of some tribal mark by which they would be recognised and admitted among the outlaws, like the mark of he sacred frigate bird on the hand, or the pierced nose, which were mentioned in a previous chapter.

---

[1] *Folk-Lore*, vol. xxvi., p. 93.
[2] Sir J. G. Frazer, *Belief in Immortality*, vol. i., p. 300.

Similar customs in other places appear to indicate that, as the outlaws visited the settlement to satisfy their material wants, so the survivors visited the outlaws to obtain help in trouble. The Eastern Melanesians think that living people can go down to the land of the dead and return alive to the upper world. Sometimes they do this in the body, but at other times only in the spirit, when they are asleep or in a faint. When the living thus make their way to the spirit land, they are sometimes cautioned by friendly ghosts to eat nothing there.[1] In Northern Melanesia the spirits of the dead are supposed to go to a far off land over the sea called *Matana nion*. Two living friends accompany him. On their arrival in the far country betel-nut is presented to them all, but the two living men refuse it because if they took it they would return no more to the land of the living.[2] The aborigines of Cape Bedford, in Queensland, believe that the souls of the dead usually leave their haunts in the forests and caves at night. Stout-hearted old men can see and converse with them, and receive from them warnings of danger, but women and children fear these spirits and never see them. The soul

---

[1] Sir J. G. Frazer, *Belief in Immortality*, vol. i., p. 355.
[2] *Ibid.*, p. 404.

of a dead man's father or friend may bear h'm
company on a journey and warn him of an
ambuscade.[1]   Again, " Nicander says that the
Celts went by night to the tombs of great men
to obtain oracles, so much did they believe that
they were still living there.   In Ireland, oracles
were also sought by sleeping on funeral cairns,
and it was to the grave of Fergus that two bards
resorted in order to obtain from him the lost story
of the *Tain*."[2]   That the tradition is not dead
even in civilized countries is proved by the
published accounts of spiritualistic séances.

The idea of mutual assistance lies at the root of
worship which consists mainly of offerings and
petitions.   It has been pointed out by many
writers that the gods appear to need their worshippers as much as the worshippers need their
gods.   Among the Amazulu it is the father of
the family who is the principal object of worship,
and if there is illness in the village, the eldest
son reproves his dead father, saying, " Let us
all die that we may see into whose house you will
enter.   You will eat grasshoppers, you will
no longer be invited to go anywhere if you destroy
your own village.", *i.e.*, if you neglect us and let
us die you will be the loser, for there will be no

---

[1] Sir J. G. Frazer. *Belief in Immortality*. vol. i., p. 130.
[2] MacCulloch. *Religion of the Ancient Celts*, p. 340.

one to invite you or feed you."[1]   In the Papuan
island of Tanna, where the gods are the spirits
of departed ancestors, a prayer after the offering
of first-fruits is spoken aloud by the chief who
acts as high priest to the silent assembly:
" Compassionate father !   Here is some food for
you ; eat it ; be kind to us on account of it."[2]

The Tami of New Guinea make offerings to the
kani or ghosts of the dead whenever they require
their assistance.   Yet the memory of ancestors
does not reach far back ; the people occupy
themselves only with the souls of those relatives
whom they have personally known.   Hence the
worship seldom extends beyond the grandfather,
even when a knowledge of more remote progenitors survives.[3]   Here we see clearly the
intention.   It would have been useless to ask a
dead outlaw for advice, but a living one might
be persuaded by a gift of food to help a relative
in trouble.   This distinction occurs frequently.
In the western islands of the Torres Straits the
people appear to distinguish the ghost of the
recently departed (*mari*) from the spirits of those
who have been longer dead (*markai*).[4]   The
Australian aborigines regard with fear the ghosts

[1] *Handbook of Folk-Lore*, p. 85.
[2] Tylor, *Primitive Culture*, vol. ii., p. 364.
[3] Sir J. G. Frazer, *Belief in Immortality*, vol. i., p. 298.
[4] *Ibid*, p. 173.

of those who just died, while they are either indifferent to the spirits of those who have died many years ago, or even look upon them as beings of higher powers than their descendants whom they benefit in various ways.[1]

Sir J. G. Frazer, *Belief in Immortality*, vol. i., p. 173.

CHAPTER XV.

CONCURRENT METHODS OF BURIAL.

It is not unusual to find, even among quite primitive people, two methods of disposing of the dead practised concurrently. For example, Colonel Mackay discovered both interment and tree-burial among the Papuans.[1] "Halting at Kurogaru we saw a grave covered with sticks (to keep off the pigs) set just beside a house. Others again bury their dead right under their huts.. . . . Other mountain tribes keep the body in the house, smoking it, while the nearest relatives watch by the bier day and night for three months, singing the while in mournful chants the dead man's life story. Then the mummy is taken into the forest and put on a platform. A feast is held in the village, from which they all march with torches, and saying : " We have done all we could for you, so harm us not," leave their dead in the silence of the trees."

All history tends to prove that man is an adaptive rather than an inventive creature :

[1] *Across Papua*, Colonel Kenneth Mackay, chap. x., p. 142 (Witherby, 1909).

he modifies old customs to meet new conditions, or borrows those of his neighbours. So, when we find in the same area two systems of disposing of the dead, we may with reasonable certainty assume a mixture or a union of two distinct peoples. Sometimes the dividing line is clearly defined, as among the Angoni of British Central Africa among whom the corpses of Chiefs are burned with all their household belongings, but the bodies of commoners are buried in caves. [1] As a hereditary ruling caste usually implies conquest, we appear to find in this example the conqueror and the conquered each retaining his old custom.

A more doubtful example occurs among the Kolosh or Tlingit Indians of Alaska who burn their ordinary dead, but deposit the bodies of Shamans in large coffins, which are supported on four posts. [2] In this instance the Shaman appears to represent an intrusive civilisation, but it may be merely another example of the conservative tendency of religion, the Shaman retaining the older custom after the rest of the population adopted cremation.

Sometimes when conquest is very complete the invader may force his custom, together with his religion, upon the conquered, but the reverse

[1] Sir J. G. Frazer, *Belief in Immortality*, vol. i., p. 162.
[2] Sir J. G. Frazer, *Belief in Immortality*, vol. i., p. 162.

of this appears to be more frequent. It is the conquered who usually takes the part of the enzyme in what chemists call catalytic action : the invader changes, the aborigine remains unchanged. Nor is this surprising ; for in new surroundings the ancient custom of the invader may prove inconvenient or even quite impracticable.

In parts of India we may see to-day the practice of cremation being reluctantly discarded. Deforestation, due to the increase of population, has raised the price of wood until the poorer classes cannot afford enough to burn the body ; so a few sticks are lighted under the corpse which is then cast, merely singed, into the Ganges.

Among some races who have adopted cremation the custom of burial is still retained for certain persons. The ancient Mexicans, as do the Gurkhas, buried those who died of infectious diseases, the Malayalis those who die of cholera or small-pox. Here we appear to find the memory of the shelter provided for the sick man who might recover ; for even during the most violent epidemics the disease is only fatal to a proportion of those who are attacked.

In India it is often the age of the deceased that determines the mode of burial. The Komars bury the young but burn the old. The Coorgs bury boys under sixteen (and also women) but burn men. In Southern India and Berar among various castes or tribes the bodies of married people are burned while those of unmarried are buried. Among others the old are burned, the young are buried. As marriage takes place at an early age the fact of being unmarried implies youth. As already mentioned, the Gurkhas usually cremate their dead,-but children under the age of twelve are buried. The Bhotias of the Himalayas bury children whose permanent teeth have not appeared but burn all others. The Grihya Sutras, the ancient Hindu law-book, lays down that children under two should be buried, and the Malayalis of Malabar adhere to this although they burn all others except those who die of cholera or smallpox. In spite of the variations due to the lapse of time we seem to find in these examples, taken all together, vague memories of the old idea that the young and vigorous, when temporarily incapacitated, should be put into shelter till they recover, while the old who are of no more use to the community need have no trouble taken about them.

The examples quoted appear to retain some slight evidence of their origin and development, but others afford no clue to guide our speculations. Why, for example, do the Chukchansi Indians

of California burn only those who die of violence
or of snake-bite, and bury all others ?   We may
imagine a nomad tribe inhabiting a region infested
with poisonous snakes and constantly at war
with their neighbours, whose earliest method of
disposing of their dead was by cremation.   If
at a later period they adopted the custom of
burial they may have retained the earlier cremation for the two kinds of death which were
commonest in their former state.   But this is
mere guess-work, for we know nothing of their
ancient history nor even which practice was the
earlier, burial or cremation.

Why, again, do the Minnetaree Indians bury
bad and quarrelsome men while good men are
laid on scaffolds ? [1]   This moral discrimination
we find echoed among some tribes of Central
Australia who usually bury young men, as well
as women and children, in trees, but not any
young man who has violated the tribal law by
taking as a wife a woman who is forbidden to
him.   He is treated like very old people and
buried in the ground. [2]   The difference according
to Messrs. Spencer and Gillen, is due to the fact
that the very infirm who cannot take part in
ceremonies which the people believe to be closely

[1] Sir J. G. Frazer, *Belief in Immortality*, vol. i., p. 162.
[2] *Ibid.*, p. 161.

concerned with the welfare of the tribe, need have no respect paid to their remains. But they are afraid of hurting the feelings of any strong man who might injure them, while they hope that the spirits of dead children and women will soon return and undergo reincarnation. Here again we do not know which custom is the older ; but while burial in the ground has acquired the idea of finality, local belief still connects tree-burial with the possibility of return

CHAPTER XVI.

TREE BURIAL.

A superstition widely diffused, which has hitherto been proof against all attempts to account for its origin, is the belief in the curative powers of holes in trees and rocks. A volume might easily be filled with instances, but as they vary little in form a few examples taken from Kelly's *Curiosities* [1] will serve to furnish the needed data.

" There stood in the village of Selbourne in Gilbert White's time ' a row of pollard ashes, which,' he says, ' by the seams and long circatrices down their sides, manifestly show that in former times they have been cleft asunder. These trees, when young and flexible, were severed and held open by wedges, while ruptured children, stripped naked, were pushed through the apertures, under a persuasion that by such a process the poor babies would be cured of their infirmity.' . . . This mode of cure has not yet gone quite out of use in England so far as the ash

---

[1] Kelly, *Curiosities of Indo-European Tradition*, p. 153 (Chapman and Hall, 1863).

is concerned, and it is still a practice much in
vogue in the southern counties, when children
are suffering from whooping cough and some
other complaints, to make them pass through the
loop formed by a bramble which has taken root
at both ends. This custom, and that of passing
children and cattle through perforated earth or
rocks or through natural or artificial openings in
trees, especially the ash and the oak, is common
to most European countries. In our own it
appears to have been no unusual thing in Saxon
times for women who were troubled with crying
brats to dig a hole in the ground and make a
tunnel through which they dragged the poor
little squallers. There was a bushy oak near
Wittstock in Altmark, the branches of which had
grown together again at some distance from the
stem, leaving open spaces between them. Who-
ever crept through these spaces was freed from
his malady whatever it might be, and many
crutches lay about which had been thrown away
by visitors to the tree who no longer needed them.
Close to the road passing through the forest of
Sullingswald there was an aged oak with a hole
shaped like the eye of a needle in a hugh stem.
This gave the foresters and charcoal burners a
welcome opportunity for hanselling strangers
who passed that way, that is to say, forcing

them to pay a small sum if they did not wish to
be dragged through the needle's eye. This
custom of hanselling travellers kept its ground
after the belief in the healing virtue of the tree
had died out."

After considering Grimm's suggestion that this
creeping through an oak-cleft seems a transference
of the malady or bewitchment to the genius of
the tree, Kelly discards it only to surrender to
Liebrecht's explanation that the whole proceeding
was originally designed to symbolise the new
birth of the patient, who, coming naked again
into the world left all his former maladies behind
him.   We may at once reject this fantastic idea
for the sufficient reason that no primitive custom
ever was originally designed to symbolise anything.   Primitive customs supplied the pressing
needs of primitive life, and it was not until these
needs had passed away, and with them the
practical value of the custom, that man had any
need to speculate about them.   The folk-lore of
tree-burial, which tradition shows had very much
the same history as interment, gives us a clue
to the origin of the custom.   Among forest-
dwellers the trees offered an ever present refuge
from danger, and spreading branches or hollow
boles served in turn as refuge, dwelling, store-
room, prison and a grave.   Putting the sick

child into the hollow of the tree or rock, or dragging it through a tunnel in the ground— which last may represent the sloping entrance to the underground dwelling—merely imitates the act of putting it out of harm's way. Originally the sick child, that could not look after itself, was placed for safety in the tree ; and the idea of recovery thus connected with the hollow tree became confused, when trees ceased to be a refuge and with a vague idea that in some way this ancient custom would effect a cure. This confusion of recovery with cure is not uncommon even in the present day ; for we credit a physician with curing us when all he does is to give us a chance of recovery. Nature effects the cure, though we, in our ignorance credit the doctor whose only action is to give nature the opportunity she needs.

The use of hollow boles of trees as a refuge or dwelling is exemplified by Frau Holda's tree, a common name in Germany for old, decayed boles. Frau Holda is described in a Hessian legend as having, in front, the form of a beautiful woman, and behind, that of a hollow tree with a rugged bark.[1] Here we have a vivid thumb-nail sketch of a woman taking shelter in a hollow tree.

[1] *Ibid.*, p. 92.

Ancient folk-lore is full of reminiscences of tree dwellers.   Yggdrasil of the Norsemen was an ash (Norse, *askr*) the tree out of which the gods formed the first man, who was thence called Askr.[1]

The descent of men from trees appears to have been a popular belief in Italy and in Greece.

Haec nemora idigenæ Fauni Nymphæque tenebant
Gensque virum truncis et duro robore nata.
Aen. viii., 314.

These woods were first the seat of sylvan powers,
Of nymphs and fauns, and savage men, who took
Their birth from trunks of trees and stubborn oak.
Dryden.

Quippe aliter tunc orbe novo coeloque recenti
Vivebant homines, qui rupto robore nati,
Compositive luto, nullos habuere parentes.
Juvenal, Sat. vi., 11.

For when the world was new, the race that broke,
Unfathered, from the soil or opening oak,
Lived most unlike the men of later times.
Gifford.

The disguised hero of the Odyssey is asked to state his pedigree, since he must needs have one, " for belike you are not come of the oak told of in old times, nor of the rock."

The practice of leaving food and weapons in or near the tree where the dead are buried bears the same construction as in the case of interment. They were originally put there for the use of the sick or injured man.   The Turrbal tribe of Southeast Australia, who deposited their dead in the

---

[1] Kelly, *Curiosities of Indo-European Tradition,* p. 141.

torks of trees, used to leave a spear and club near the corpse that the spirit of the dead might have weapons wherewith to kill game for his sustenance in the future state. A yam-stick was placed in the ground at a woman's grave so that she might go away at night and seek for roots.[1] Similarly we find the belief that ghosts haunt the trees where the dead are buried. The aborigines of the Pennefather River Queensland, believe that all disembodied human spirits wander about in the bush, but there are certain hollow trees or clumps of trees with wide spreading branches, which they most love to haunt.[2] In India it is a common belief that old *pipul* trees are often haunted by the spirits of men of ancient times who used to live in them. At the foot of such a tree it is usual to build a small shrine on which lights are burned and floral offerings are placed, and it is considered dangerous to pass by it in the dark for fear of being carried off by the spirit. It has already been shown that these beliefs record the period when the outcasts lived in their shelters on the outskirts of the settlement.

The custom of temporary outlawry of the unfit, followed by exile to the older settlement, was

[1] Sir J. G. Frazer, *Belief in Immortality*, vol. i., p. 146 (Macmillan, 1913).
[2] *Ibid*, vol. i., p. 128.

dealt with in chapter five. As then shown, it is illustrated to-day by the practice of placing the coffin which contains the body among the branches of a tree. This custom has been discovered to exist, not only in the Babar archipelago, but also in Egypt; and it is from the latter country that light is thrown on our modern European practice of interment combined with the coffin and the shell. Flinders Petrie tells that coffins hollowed out of a single block, to fit the outline of the mummy, were used in all the earlier periods. In later times such forms were built up of boards." [1] This appears to indicate a tendency to economise wood. We may surmise that at first the body was placed in the hollow trunk of a tree, then that the tree was cut up into several sections each sufficient for one body, and finally that the more economical method of using planks was adopted. Connected with this is the European custom of putting the body in a shell inside the coffin. Thus we record the underground refuge by the practice of interment, and the tree-trunk refuge of the forest-dweller by using the shell. The coffin may represent a boat, and so record the departure over water. The use of the same word for boat

[1] *The Arts and Crafts of Ancient Egypt*, chap. xiii. (Foulis, 1909).

and coffin by the Olo Ngadjoe of south-east Borneo[1] suggests that this is so, but unsupported by further indications it remains in the region of speculation.

[1] Chap. v., *supra.*

CHAPTER XVII

MOURNING.

The difficulty always hitherto experienced in harmonising the numerous and highly varied customs of mourning is due in great measure to the fact that ceremonies whose original purposes were quite distinct have been thrust indiscriminately into one category. In the Handbook of Folk-Lore they are summed up thus : [1]

" Typically, it (mourning) consists of creating a marked contrast to the mourners ordinary appearance. Those who habitually shave, let their hair grow, those who plait it and bind it up, let it fall in dishevelled locks, and *vice versa*. Sometimes the mourning relatives discard clothes altogether and bedaub themselves with paint, or cut off a finger joint, or gash their bodies with knives and let the blood flow over the grave. Often they must fast, or at least refrain from cooking food, until the funeral."

Here we find three classes of mourning rites, to which may be added wailing and food taboos,

[1] *Handbook of Folk-Lore*, p. 213.

all filed away together and ticketed : Mourning for the Dead. Before any progress in this line of enquiry can be made the first step is to recognise that the title is misleading. It is generally recognised that the majority of mourning customs are protective in their nature, and by their due observance men ward off vague, unspecified evils that superstition connects fearfully with a dead person. But though these evils are imaginary now, there was a time when they were real ; for superstition is the shadow cast by dangers long forgotten. Cain, after slaying his brother Abel, went and dwelt in the land of Nod, and precautions that have now degenerated into useless ceremonies were taken in earlier times under the impulse of stern necessity. But though the customs were essentially protective we have no grounds for the assumption that they were always, or even generally, a defence against the dead. Primitive men of modern times may practice them with that idea, but they have less to guide their speculations than we who can compare the rites and superstitions of many races.

From previous chapters it will at once be evident that among the dangers which threatened the living was the anger of the so-called dead, that is, of those under sentence of exile or outlawry.

But whole classes of these customs appear rather to have been directed against living foes. These, properly speaking, do not come within the scope of this work for they are not concerned with the " dead " either in the sense of outlaws or as really dead ; but as hitherto they have been grouped with other funeral customs, and thereby have caused misunderstanding and confusion, it is necessary to define their scope and intention.

It has been recognised that at the foundation of those customs which involve a change of appearance there lies the idea of disguise, but it is now generally admitted that, as an attempt to deceive the ghost of the dead man, they offer many incongruities. It is not necessary to quote examples because the assumption that the disguise was originally intended to deceive the ghost is without foundation. It is another instance of the common mistake of deciding on the verdict first, taking the evidence next, and then trying to find arguments to prove the verdict right. We begin with the fixed idea that these customs are " mourning for the dead." and at once find ourselves in difficulties ; for disguise is not as a rule concerned with the dead except quite indirectly. One of these exceptions is quoted by Hartland. [1] " A practice occasionally in use

[1] *Ritual and Belief*, p. 254.

among the Herero is when a dying man intimates
to one of his relatives, who crowd round him at
such a time, that he has ' decided upon taking
him away after his death,' that is to say, that he
will kill him (fetch him to the other world),
the person so threatened has recourse to a witch
doctor. This functionary strips him, washes and
greases him afresh, and dresses him in other
clothes. He is now quite at his ease about the
threatening of death caused by the deceased ;
for, says he, ' Now our father does not know me.' "

In explanation of this custom a reference may
be made to the earlier chapter in which the
reasons were discussed for the slaughter of
retainers and the burial of a widow with the
deceased husband. It records the proprietary
right of the outlaw over his dependents, his claim
to be accompanied by them into exile, and
also the very natural reluctance of the dependents
to submit to the rule.

But, as Hartland admits, this is quite an
exceptional instance. Mourning disguise can
rarely be explained as an attempt to deceive
the ghost : nor was that its motive. Disguise
was adopted to deceive the living. An attack
or raid by one tribe or portion of a tribe, upon
another ordinarily involved retaliation, and
though the actual offenders might not be

recognised, the tribe to which they belonged was evident from their dress and tribal marks.   Even in the present day the law of the blood-feud does not always demand the blood of the slayer. Honour and justice are satisfied if revenge is taken upon one of his family or clan.   The whole tribe or clan being thus in danger of reprisals their aim was to avoid recognition, and one obvious precaution was to change their distinctive dress and tribal marks.   Disguise, then, was a *ruse de guerre* adopted as a means of evading recognition and consequent reprisals.   So the mark put upon Cain when he cried :   Every man that finds me shall slay me, was probably a tribal mark, different from his own, thereby affording him some chance of escape.

According to Sir J. Frazer the fear of being haunted is the reason for the destruction of property.   In Mabuiag, one of the western islands of the Torres Straits " on the day of death the mourners went into the gardens, slashed at the taro, knocked down coconuts, pulled up sweet potatoes, and destroyed bananas.   We are told that the food was destroyed for the sake of the dead man, it was ' like saying good-bye.'   We may suspect that the real motive for the destruction was the same as that for laying food and water beside the corpse, namely, a wish to give the ghost no excuse for returning to haunt and pester his surviving relatives." [1] Substituting outlaws for ghosts this is the same explanation as has been given in an earlier chapter. But there may have been yet another reason for the adoption of this custom. Death resulting usually from feuds and quarrels during which the possessions of the weaker party doubtless were destroyed, it is not impossible that, in later times this destruction was continued as protective mimicry—the transition occurring in this manner. A defeated community, after war and the destruction of its property by the victor, suffered great privations. It was then even more than usually imperative to cast out the weaker members whom they could not support, including men injured in the battle. Ordinarily these outlaws had an acknowledged right to some measure of support; but the results of the battle had made this obviously impossible and the survivors were therefore relieved of their responsibility. The advantage was obvious, and it is not impossible that a judicious, but not excessive destruction of property was first practised to deceive the outlaws, and afterwards as an indication that the community refused to support them.

It must be remembered that among primitive

[1] *Belief in Immortality*, vol. i., p. 174 (Macmillan 1913).

people death from old age was unknown.
Dangers were too many. For the most part
they must have died in fights with men and
beasts, or from accidents. Disease may have
carried off some, but in those hard times it is
unlikely that those who were weak from sickness
were able to escape a violent death. It seems
probable that the vast majority of deaths occurred
in quarrels, in battles, or from the attacks of
wild beasts ; and in such cases when one was
killed it is unlikely that his companions escaped
unhurt unless they deserted him. The memory
of this is preserved among many nations who
include among their other funeral rites that
of laceration or even mutilation of their bodies.
Spencer and Gillen report that among the War-
ramunga of Central Australia the women fight
with one another and cut each other's scalps,
while all near relations of the deceased cut their
own skulls open with yam-sticks.[1] Among the
Arawaks the men of the village assemble and
scourge one another with whips until the blood
runs and strips of skin and muscle hang down,
while some die of their wounds.[2] Among the
Fijians a finger-joint is cut off to indicate
mourning, and this is also done among the

[1] Spencer and Gillen, *The Native Tribes of Central Australia*,
p. 521.
[2] Hartland, *Ritual and Belief*, p. 262.

aborigines of Montana (U.S.A.)[1] Certain races
appear to have allowed this custom to fall into
disuse, but still represent it in mimicry. So
the Skgomic tribe paint the breasts of their
garments with red paint and the widow has red
streaks painted on the crown of her head. In
some parts of West Australia they cover their
heads with red mud. And on the Ivory Coast
some tribes mark different parts of their bodies
with red earth.[2] It is almost impossible to doubt
that the red colouring is intended to represent
blood, thus implying the modification of an
earlier and more brutal custom.

Not only was it likely that the companions
of the man who was killed were injured in the
fray, but human nature being what it is, they
must have been anxious to let the rest of the
tribe know that they had suffered; their wounds
redounded to their credit. It would have been a
shameful thing not to have been wounded. Thus
injury to the survivors came to be considered as
something due to the dead.

It seems, then, that mutilation or its mimicry
is a relic of the times when honourable wounds
were proof that the bearer had done his duty,
whereas unwounded he might be thought traitor,
deserter, or a coward.

[1] Williams, *Fiji and Fijians*, p. 169.
[2] Hartland, *Ritual and Belief*, p. 237.

After describing the severity with which Australian tribes cut their bodies and burn themselves at the funeral of a dead man, Sir J. G. Frazer explains that " everything is regulated by certain definite rules ; a woman who did not thus maul herself when she ought to do so would be very severely punished, or even killed, by her brother.   Similarly with men, it is only those who stand in certain relationships to the deceased who must cut and hack themselves in this manner."[1]

We next come to a group of practices whose origin appears to be entirely connected with war, and one example will suffice to indicate their general nature.   At Wagawaga and Tubetube in British New Guinea " during the first two or three weeks after a funeral the relatives may not eat boiled food, but only roast ; they may not drink water but only the milk of young coconuts, and although they may eat yams, they must abstain from bananas and sugar-cane."[2]

These taboos, as also the customs of celebacy and fasting, indicate that those who had been engaged in battle were excluded from the tribe as long as their presence might involve them in the reprisals which the enemy might be expected to take.   Living for the time being outside the

[1] *Belief in Immortality*, vol. i., p. 157 (Macmillan, 1913).
[2] *Ibid.*, vol. i., p. 208.

community access to their women was impossible, they no doubt suffered from want of food : they were dependent on what could be gathered in the forest, and debarred from the produce of the village gardens ; while such food as they were able to obtain must be eaten raw or roasted, for without cooking pots it could not be boiled.

Finally we come to the almost universal custom of wailing for the dead. This consists of calling repeatedly upon the dead by name in a voice despairing and at the same time penetrating. It is usually performed by women, who appear to represent the dependents of the outlaw, deprived of their supporter, calling upon him to return. Excessively prolonged grief appears to have been discouraged, and this is intelligible if we consider that the return of the outlaw was opposed to the wishes and interests of the wishes and interests of the community. According to the folk-lore of many people it has a bad effect upon the dead themselves. In *Redgauntlet* Sir Walter Scott says, " The belief was general throughout Scotland that the excessive lamentation over the loss of friends disturbed the repose of the dead, and broke even the rest of the grave." In a Serbian popular song it is said that a sister wept incessantly over her brother's grave, but her tears at last became intolerable to the deceased, because he was detained on earth by her excessive grief, and suffered great torment. [1] The explanation appears to be that the outlaw, called by his dependents, was tempted to violate his sentence of outlawry and return to the settlement, or refuse to undertake the journey to the older colony.

[1] W. K. Kelly, *Curiosities of Indo-European Tradition*. p. 127, quoting Talvj, i., 274, 1st edit. (Chapman and Hall. 1863).

CHAPTER XVIII.

RELICS OF VOLUNTARY OUTLAWRY.

So far we have considered mainly the sufferings of those who were driven out of the community, but it is likely, more especially in later times, that exile had its compensations. Possessing no property the outlaws had no reason to fear attack : they were not obliged to undertake the severe manual labour by which the peasant earns his living. And, as was shown in the previous chapter, the attitude of the tribe towards them gradually became more benevolent. This doubtless showed itself in larger and more frequent offerings of food. Thus in time their condition became at least endurable.

We can understand, then, that men who were not strong enough to take their part in war and in the peasants' daily toil, as also those of a more peaceful or contemplative nature, may have preferred the mitigated hardships of voluntary exile to the turbulence and exhausting labour of ordinary life. These may have been the forerunners of the anchorites and hermits of more recent times, as the latter found successors in our modern monks and nuns.

Many indications lead to this conclusion. As we have seen already, those who became a burden to their fellow men were driven out to live apart until they died : the monk is dead to the world. Certain things were done which in time hardened into funeral rites : the final ceremony in the making of a monk or nun is the funeral service. Neither own property beyond their absolute needs. The outlaw dwelt in his refuge, suffered from hunger and cold : the monk has a bare cell without a fire even in winter, and is subject to frequent fasts : he is also sometimes under a vow of silence which is mimicry of isolation. The outlaw was dependent to a great extent on offerings of food : the religious institutions are supported by charity. The Buddhist monks in Burma wander round the village early every morning in silence carrying a dish into which the charitably inclined put a spoonful of rice : the outlaw as we have seen, came by night to gather food that was left. Here again silence represents isolation, and the outlaw was careful to avoid observation. Finally, as we have seen, the elder outlaws were the holders of the traditions of the tribe and all the ancient knowledge : the monastic orders, and later, the universities which were closely connected with them, kept alight the lamp of learning — but it was the ancient learning. Even until quite recently the universities, true descendants of the outlaws of the neolithic age, cared only for Greek and Latin, the ancient learning, and left to the outer world all that more nearly concerns material progress.

We see then, a double change come over the ancient custom. With increasing prosperity men ceased to drive away the injured and infirm, but preserved relics of the old conditions in their burial rites. On the other hand ' outlawry ' became voluntary and those who took it on themselves took up with it the old traditions.

We have also what may be yet another relic of voluntary outlawry, and that is suicide. I suggest this with diffidence, even with doubt, and merely offer for more mature consideration a few facts that appear to lend countenance to the hypothesis.

Self maiming is and always has been, as far as we know, a common method of avoiding the dangers and hardships of war. In modern armies it is treated as one of the graver military offences and we have no reason to suppose that it was viewed with less disapprobation in early times. On the other hand it is generally difficult to prove that the injury was self-inflicted. Whether it was so or not, the man was a useless burden and presumably was cast out. I suggest, tentatively, that as the burial of the dead is one of the surviving forms of the provision of a refuge for the injured, so suicide may be one of the survivals of self-maiming. In its early stage it was an attempt to evade obligations to the community. But if the injury was not severe enough to make a man useless it failed in its effect—he would not be outlawed—and outlawry, as has been shown, was not in later times without advantages. On the other hand if the injury was too severe he died ; and, if desperate, his tendency would be to err on the side of severity. In either event he escaped something that he could not face, and suicide has always borne the stigma of cowardice. As has just been mentioned the object was to evade an obligation to the community, an obligation that in early times must have been very pressing—to take his share of their dangers and their hardships. Exclusion from the tribe was the punishment, and attempted suicide is still punishable by imprisonment, that is to say, by exclusion from society, although it is no longer an act that affects the public welfare. A man may offend against himself in any other way, he may ruin his health and dissipate his fortune, thus becoming a burden to the state, and yet not offend against the law. But he must not make an attempt upon his own life, even though he would thereby relieve the state of the burden of maintaining him.

One other point requires to be mentioned, namely, the popular belief that the ghosts of suicides are restless like those of men who have died violent deaths. The reason appears to be that the society of outlaws resented the intrusion of one who would be a burden to them, and who was therefore compelled to haunt the precincts of the community to obtain food.

I have not attempted to discuss the matter fully, and no doubt a study of the special burial rites would throw more light upon it. The point I wish to make is that man is the only animal that takes its own life. At what stage in his career did he begin, or from what other practice was it developed? The combination of self-maiming and outlawry appears to offer at least a reasonable solution of the mystery.

CHAPTER XIX.

Man reluctantly discards anything that has proved useful to him, so when he began to live above the ground he still retained his underground dwelling and made his new home on the top of it. He found the old one useful for storing his grain and other valuables and in course of time it developed into a thesaurus or treasury. If about this time the cattle also were lodged above the ground the sloping entrance was no longer needed. With only the one entrance at the top, it was impossible to get out of it without the aid of a ladder, so a further use was discovered for it : it became a prison. " Dr. Corssen deals with the use as prisons of structures analogous to Mycenæan beehive-tombs. He cites the many and mostly familiar mythological instances of underground prisons, Danæ, Lycurgus, Ephialtes, etc. A historical case of such a dungeon, that of Philopoemen, is of special interest because the dungeon was actually

called a Thesaurus." [1]   It was in such a ' grave '
that the guilty Vestal was buried alive.   Plutarch
writes :   " The disgraced virgin was buried alive
beside the gate Kolline at which is a precipice
within the city stretching far under the earth.
It is called a sepulchral mound in the Latin tongue.
Here a subterranean dwelling is prepared, not very
large, having an entrance from above.   In this
is placed a bed spread out and a lamp burning,
the beginnings of the sacrifice, and a few things
necessary for life, such as bread, water in a pail,
milk, oil, as expiatory offerings.   The body
perished by hunger."   The victim was first
carried in procession, then the chief priest " brings
her out covered up and they place her on a ladder
leading into the house below . . . the ladder
was raised again and the dwelling was hidden
from view by much earth being placed on it from
above so that the place was level with the rest
of the mound." [2]

The growth of humanitarian ideas has resulted
in recent times and in civilized countries in a
great improvement in prison administration.
But originally the prisoner was a person whom,
in the interests of the community, it was necessary to get rid of—and to get rid of once and for

---

[1] J. E. Harrison, in *Essays to Ridgeway*, p. 152.
[2] *Ibid.*, p. 144 *et seq.*

all.   But the custom of the blood-feud, the earliest
form of law, made execution impossible without
throwing upon relations the duty of retaliation.
So the ancient custom was retained of providing
the undesirable person with food for his immediate
needs, and putting him in a safe place—with this
difference, that he could not escape from his
shelter.   That he would die there was obvious,
but so did the great majority of the old, infirm,
and injured who from time immemorial had
been cast out by the community.   The old and
recognised custom included no bloodshed and
therefore involved no blood-feud.

CHAPTER XX.

We have travelled far from the grotto where lay the bones of palæolithic men with weapons and the remnants of their food beside them. For we have seen the progenitors of the human race, born of the trees or of the rocks, lived with our ancestors in their underground dwellings, and learned the secrets of the Egyptian pyramids, and the meaning of Moslem minarets and domes. We have sailed with dead Vikings in a burning ship, stood by when widows were buried alive, and witnessed the agony of an Indian suttee. We have been spectators of the Deluge watched while Lost Atlantis sank beneath the waves, and heard the church bells ringing in the submerged City of Is. With the Druids we have sent letters to departed friends, and paid the debts we owed them when they were alive. Suicides and children unbaptised have told us why they cannot rest in peace. Ghosts and

vampires have been our companions of the
night, and we have fled with them at cock-crow
to the land of shades.   We know why dead men
cast no shadow, and why they suffer from hunger
and from cold.   We have visited the dwellings
of the dead—our foreheads stained with ginger,
or the mark of the sacred frigate-bird upon ou
hands, to gain for us admission—and have
declined the food their hospitality offered lest
we should not be suffered to return.   We have
watched a dead man rise from his oriented grave,
and after paying Charons obolus, have traced his
footsteps to the other world.   There we have
seen him in his life, and stood beside him when
he died the second death.

In bringing the enquiry to a close I am conscious
how inadequate has been the treatment of a
subject so vast and varied.   Want of access
to a library, want of leisure, and want of detailed
knowledge have all been contributary causes.
Some debatable points should have been argued
at more length, and illuminated by a greater
wealth of illustration ;   while many important
aspects of burial have been omitted altogether.

Cremation, for example, has been mentioned
only incidentally.   It may have been adopted
when population became more dense, and the
danger of infection was realised.   But we have

no right to assume this ; nor does it explain how
the idea was discovered, only how it spread. It
is not enough to say that it was adopted in
imitation of some intrusive or neighbouring
race, for this is but to put the difficulty farther
back, and fails entirely to explain why men
first began to burn. the bodies of their dead.
If customs grow, and do not start their life full
fledged, we must look for yet an earlier custom.
Enquiry may show that cremation originated
among people dwelling in regions where forest
and prairie fires were common, and, it may be,
not only were the dead disposed of thus, but
perhaps the sick and injured also were left behind
to be burned. The burning of offerings to the
dead may have followed naturally when cremation
was substituted for interment ; but it is doubtful
whether this explanation, even if correct in some
instances, covers the whole field. Sir J. G.
Frazer asks whether the idea is " by volatilising
the solid substance of the food, to make it more
accessible to the thin unsubstantial nature of
the ghost."[1] Although this may be the current
belief among savages it postulates much previous
speculation ; and speculation usually follows
action, not precedes it. He offers an alternative
suggestion that offerings were destroyed to

[1] *Belief in Immortality*, vol. i., p. 349.

deprive the ghost of any excuse for returning to claim them. This is far more reasonable and fits in with other methods of destruction that are carried out with that express intention. We must, however, bear in mind that roasting was probably the earliest form of cookery. No vessels are required, and an animal can be roasted whole upon a fire. There is perhaps an element of truth in Lamb's tale of the origin of roast pig. So it may be that to throw morsels of food upon the fire is a relic, now become a rite, of the far off time when an injured man was given a supply of roasted meat to support him till he recovered; and the burning of other property may well have been only an extension of this idea.

Among subjects that have not been touched is the common belief in a plurality of souls. When ancient customs became extinct and were utterly forgotten, there remained traditional beliefs connected with the dead. There was something that hovered about the tomb, something that needed food, something that occasionally visited the living furtively by night, something that was dangerous unless propitiated or frightened. These were all near by. But there was also something that went on a long journey to a distant land—a land that it would never reach unless instructed how to find the way. And the very words originally used to describe the various conditions of the dead may have survived in mangled form, but with their early associations clinging to them like wet garments that conceal the body but reveal the form. These vague traditions, told in separate stories unconnected with each other yet all mysteriously related to the dead, had to be explained somehow to fit in with what men knew. And they knew that dead men did not breathe, and that dead bodies decayed and turned to dust. Thus a mingling of tradition and fact resulted in strange theories.

The belief in two or more souls, one of which remains, at least for a time in the neighbourhood of its grave, while the other travels to some distant region, is, I suggest, the record in disjointed fragments of what was once a continuous account of the condition of outlawed men. The Arunta of Central Australia bury their dead and raise a mound over the grave, but leave a depression in the mound on the side which faces towards the spot where the spirit of the deceased is supposed to have dwelt in the intervals between his successive reincarnations; and we are expressly told that the purpose of leaving the depression is to allow the spirit to go out and in easily.[1] The origin of the grave, the mound above it, and the means of going out and in have already been explained ; but in the present myth we must eliminate the Australian theory of reincarnation which arose from their ignorance of the sexual cause of birth. The belief, cleared of extraneous matter, remains thus : the depression faced in the direction where the spirit would go to dwell, that is, according to what has been shown before, the direction the man would take when sufficiently recovered to travel. Sir J. G. Frazer, quoting Messrs. Spencer and Gillen, goes on to say, " until the final ceremony of mourning has been performed at the grave, the ghost is believed to spend his time partly in watching over his near relations and partly in the company of its *Arumburinga*, or spiritual double, who lives at the old *Nanja* spot, that is, at the place where the disembodied soul tarries waiting to be born again.[2] Thus the Arunta imagine that for some time after death the spirit of the deceased is in a sort of intermediate state, partly hovering about the abode of the living, partly visiting his own spiritual home, to which on the completion of the mourning ceremonies he will retire to await the new birth." The Malagasy of Madagascar

---

[1] Sir J. G. Frazer, *Belief in Immortality*, vol. i., p. 164.
[2] Tylor, *Primitive Culture*, vol. i., p. 434.

say that the *saina* or mind vanishes at death,
the *aina* or life becomes mere air, but the *mato-atoa* or ghost hovers round the tomb. The
Algonquin of North America believe that man
has two souls, and at death one abides with the
body, and for this the survivors leave offerings
of food, while the other departs to the land of
the dead." [1]

These different souls appear to represent two
stages of the same man's life—outlawry and exile.
On first being cast out by the community he
lived close by in his shelter, and this is recorded
by the soul that dwells in or near the grave.
Then, unless he died, there followed the departure
to the older settlement which is represented by
the soul that goes to the land of the dead.

Some times, however, the belief in a double soul
may have resulted from a mixed ancestry, involving the inheritance of traditions of two different
methods of disposing of the old and injured.
The Tami, for instance, believe that every man
has two souls, a long one and a short one, both
of which survive his death ; but one of them
repairs to the lower world while the other is last
sighted off the coast of New Britain. These Tami
are people of Melanesian stock who have settled

[1] Sir J. G. Frazer, *Belief in Immortality*, vol. i., pp. 292,
296, *et seq.* (Macmillan, 1913).

in New Guinea and, like other Melanesians, intermarried with the original inhabitants, besides perhaps having an infusion of Polynesian blood. It is therefore not ulikely that they have retained their old tradition of the despatch of useless members to an earlier home beyond the sea, while adopting the local beliefs connected with the disposal of the sick in underground shelters. But this is by no means certain, for the belief may be accounted for equally well if those who were to be despatched over-sea were first put in shelter underground until the season of the year when the voyage took place. The quaint idea of the height of the ghosts throws a little more light on the subject, for although the size of Tami graves has not been described, those of the Tamos of Astrolabe Harbour in German New Guinea, a tribe who also bury their dead inside or close to their houses, are only three feet deep and four feet long, and the legs of full grown people have to be doubled up when the body is interred. Shortness may then imply a sick person crouching in a little shelter. When he was sufficiently recovered to undertake the voyage, he would stand up again and be long. The restrictions of primitive language combined with the fact that the old custom had changed and been for-gotten, would account for the confusion. It might be claimed that the idea of size is due to some earlier custom of burying only the young and disposing otherwise of full grown people. But this does not seem likely as children would not be objects of fear, nor would they be able to help the living when properly propitiated ; and both these superstitions exist. Again, " the long soul is identified with the shadow . . . when a man dies the long soul quits his body and appears to his relations at a distance. . . It then departs by way of Maligep, on the west coast of New Britain, to a village on the north coast, the inhabitants of which recognise the Tami ghosts as they flit past. . . . , The short soul tarries for a time in the neighbourhood of the body before it takes its departure for Lamboam, which is the abode of the dead in the nether world." [1]

Here we see that the long soul has a shadow and by implication the short soul has none. This absence of a shadow has already been explained : it defines those who remain in their refuges during the day and only approach the settlement by night when their approach is not so likely to be observed. The belief in the two souls appears, therefore, to be a disconnected, but once continuous, account of what happened

[1] Sir J. G. Frazer, *Belief in Immortality*, vol. i. pp. 291-2.

to the outlaw. First he stayed in his shelter, only coming out at night to hunt for food and, later, he emerged to make the voyage to the older settlement.

Besides these and many other blanks that remain to be filled in, there are numerous subjects outside the field of burial which may be eludicated ; for the present theory of burial resembles Bluebeard's key and open secret chambers. We may find, for example, the long sought explanation of the Pandora myth. The lid that was raised may have been the covering stone, not of a ‾jar, but of the underground dwelling that became a store-house, a treasury, and a grave. The want of ventilation when left unopened for some time, and the need for letting the dangerous gases escape are mentioned by Varro.[1] These might account for the misfortunes that were spread among the people. When the lid was closed again Elpis alone was left inside, and we may wonder if Elpis was the corpse.

The ancient Egyptian custom of carrying a mummy round at a feast may be a survival of feeding the outcast ; while even the mystery of the execution of kings, treated so exhaustively by Sir J. G. Frazer, may have a little indirect

[1] Miss Harrison, in *Essays to Ridgeway*, p. 141.

light cast on it by the knowledge that the outlawry of those who were useless was the origin
of the burial of the dead.

This volume opened with the suggestion that
the so-called graves of palæolithic times were
in reality not graves but temporary shelters.
Taken by itself this hypothesis appears at first
to be of little more than academic interest,
an idle speculation of small scope, beginning and
ending with the lives of men long passed away ;
and those who have laboured through succeeding
chapters may well have forgotten from what
foundation the superstructure rises. For our
enquiries have carried us into the beliefs and
practices of the present day : they have opened
up new avenues of thought, and thrown strange
light on some vexed and abstruse questions.
If the foundations prove to be firm, and the
arguments based on it are not severely shaken,
speculation will not stop here ; for lines branch
off in all directions that cannot fail to tempt
enquirers onward.

The preceding chapters make no claim to be
more than a first rough survey of a region that
has never been mapped. I have endeavoured
to explore the sources, and to trace the general
course of the main rivers of custom, and also to
indicate the more prominent landmarks ; but I

must leave details to be filled in by others more expert. It is only to be expected that later surveys will disclose inaccuracies ; but if my skeleton map is approximately correct, the errors will soon be rectified ; and it will have served its purpose if meanwhile it helps to guide lost wanderers in this vast, mysterious region.

THE END.

E. AUSTIN AND SON' PRINTERS, CLIFTON, BRISTOL.

For Product Safety Concerns and Information please contact our EU
representative GPSR@taylorandfrancis.com
Taylor & Francis Verlag GmbH, Kaufingerstraße 24, 80331 München, Germany